A Quantum Leap of

FAITH

T0001839

A Quantum Leap of
FAITH

MICHAEL SIMON BODNER, PH.D.

TATE PUBLISHING
AND **ENTERPRISES,** LLC

Published by Tate Publishing & Enterprises, LLC
127 E. Trade Center Terrace | Mustang, Oklahoma 73064 USA
1.888.361.9473 | www.tatepublishing.com

Tate Publishing is committed to excellence in the publishing industry. The company reflects the philosophy established by the founders, based on Psalm 68:11,
"The Lord gave the word and great was the company of those who published it."

Book design copyright © 2016 by Tate Publishing, LLC. All rights reserved.
Cover design by Nino Carlo Suico
Interior design by Richell Balansag

Published in the United States of America

ISBN: 978-1-68237-240-1
Religion / Science
15.10.29

This book is dedicated to my best friend and wife of twenty-six years, my wife Stacey, and my parents, Marsha and Nathan Bodner. I am who I am and what I am thanks to their love and support. My heart and soul are strong due to the support they have offered in all of my endeavors.

The most incomprehensible thing about the world
is that it is at all comprehensible.

—Albert Einstein, US (German-born) physicist
(1879–1955)

CONTENTS

INTRODUCTION

Have you ever wondered how it could be possible for us to understand, as much as we do, about the universe? Here we are, tiny assemblies of atoms and molecules, residing on a ball of rock traveling around a not very special fireball in a distant arm of a common galaxy. The universe is billions of years old and too vast for us even to imagine its size. Yet we, humankind, who have been on the scene as thinking, tool using life-forms only for a few tens of thousands of years, seem to understand a great deal.

We scientists know almost everything about the creation of the universe itself; the evolution of galaxies, stars, and planets; the beginnings of life and the evolutionary process that allow life to adapt to changing conditions. We have discovered the building blocks of nature and life itself, and in the last fifty years have entered a phase in which our knowledge will give us almost godlike powers. We can harness the power source of the stars themselves. Soon we will be able to create new living organisms and engineer existing life. Eventually, we will even be able to design our own children.

All of this understanding comes from a methodical and developing process by which the human mind and a society of individuals have come from primitive hunters to farmers to city builders and risen to become the dominant life-form on this planet. The power of the mind is unquestionable. The fact that our understanding can be extended to the edges of time and space is nothing less than miraculous. Miraculous.

Not a word usually associated with science. But then that is the point of this book. We have two separate worldviews—science and theology. Many of us are content to compartmentalize our religious and secular selves. We can accept ideas as either faith-based or rooted in reason and logic. We can accept the existence of God as a personal belief set that either accepts the image of a fatherlike God managing everything that happens or imagines a real world based upon order emerging from chaos. Indeed, the human psyche itself seems to be wired to need a religious component to help us cope with the harshness of the universe.

The dilemma for a modern thinking man is that science and theology have begun to overlap, and our ability to compartmentalize our life is failing. In cosmology, quantum mechanics, biophysics, and even cognitive psychology, the lines between faith and reason are blurred. This book attempts to present a unification of thought and vision that addresses the great divide between science and theology as well as the great overlap.

The genesis for this work lies partially in my own personal history. It was my very good fortune to grow up during the golden age of America in the city that was its crown jewel, New York. I decided as a young boy to become a scientist.

At ten years of age, my parents allowed me to take the subway all the way into Manhattan to the American Museum of Natural History by myself. There and at the Hayden Planetarium, contained on its campus, I began my journey of intellect and faith. I still remember the old planetarium. In a round dark room with very comfortable rocking chairs, an otherworldly machine rose out the floor and transported the viewer out into space and across time. The Zeiss Mark IV projector was a marvel of mechanics and optics in a time long before digital special effects and computer-generated imagery (CGI) that served as a catalytic force on thousands of young minds trying to learn about the glory of the universe. That the projector looked a little like the Martian walking machines from H. G. Wells' *The War of the Worlds* thrilled my young heart.

The Mark IV large-size projector in the planetarium of the Nagoya City science museum (Photo credit: Nagoya City science museum)	H. G. Well's Martian walkers as shown in an original *Amazing Stories* cover (*Amazing Stories*, vol. 2 (No. five), 1927

The 1950s was an amazing time to be a child. We basked in the optimism that science and technology were going to bring us a glorious world in our lifetime, coupled with the dark foreboding of the possibility of nuclear holocaust. We had science fiction and Sputnik. We believed that the future would bring us clean and cheap energy, abundant food, freedom from disease, rockets to other planets, personal computers, mini wireless communication devices, and flying cars. We all felt the power of the human mind and had faith in its unlimited potential.

No wonder I chose science.

My parents were Holocaust survivors born in Eastern Europe. My mother and father were caught up in one of the most horrific periods in civilization's history. I was born in Brooklyn, New York, and raised in the Jewish tradition. The Holocaust was a reality to us, yet my parents never spoke directly to me about any of the details. We lived in a refugee ghetto in Coney Island, surrounded by other survivors. I became aware at an early age that we were different and even shunned by the American Jews, but that is another story for another time.

My parents were religiously ambiguous. My father profoundly professed that he was a Jew, but harbored great anger at God for allowing the Holocaust to happen. My mother was thirteen when the war started, watched nearly her entire world crumble, wound up in a concentration camp, lost an arm after being shot by a Schindler's List commandant, and yet continued to believe in the goodness of people and the blessings that God had granted to our family. We practiced religion sparingly.

This was the root of my conflict. Was there a God? If so, how could He stand by and watch His people slaughtered like animals? What did it mean to be a Jew and be angry at God? Why did my mother praise God for blessings after all she had been through?

Along with these questions, which were quite deep for a preschooler, I continued to look for a framework with which I could organize my worldview. It was within the context of this quest to understand everything that I found science. Books were everywhere. I learned to read before I went to school. To me, books were miracles. At the library I was offered answers to questions that my parents could not, or would not, answer.

Where did the world come from?

How old was the universe?

How does everything work?

My appetite for books was voracious. I read everything that I could get my hands on. My mind was a sponge sucking up every piece of knowledge and wisdom that I could glean from whatever source I was able to find. I listened to adults talking, watched TV, and read newspapers. I also discovered the *jackpot of all facts*—the American Museum of Natural History, which became my favorite place to go whenever the opportunity presented itself.

I was a curious child. The world around me was a place of wonder, a place in which I constantly probed for answers. I began to show an early tendency toward scientific methodology, sometimes with dramatic results. My father was an avid Brooklyn Dodger fan. He loved to do two things when he was not working: take me outside the ballpark and listen to the Bums (as the team was known to its loving fans or watch them on TV). When an amazing advance in technology arrived in the form of a portable radio, suddenly he was able to take me to the park and listen to the game simultaneously!

The radio itself was a miracle of advanced design. It contained vacuum tubes, just like our radio and television, had a massive battery, and weighed less than fifteen pounds. My father loved this radio, as did I.

After about two weeks of listening to the games and music, my four-year-old mind ached with curiosity. While Dad was at work I decided to take the radio apart, which I did with the neatness of a very young child.

When my father got home and found the radio completely destroyed, I am sure that he was not pleased. Rather than getting angry, he and my mother sat me down and asked me why I did it. My response was simple: I told them that I wanted to see the little people in the box and play with them.

Anger gave way to something else and I imagine that they both smiled inside. I promised never to take anything apart again without asking for permission. This was a promise that I broke several times. As it turns out, my father was able to take the shattered device to the electrical appliance store and have it repaired. Indeed, in those days, they actually had people who fixed broken toasters and radios and for less than it would cost to replace them!

My parents supported my curiosity and thirst for answers, which was a very good thing. I am sure that I tried their patience on numerous occasions as I grew.

As a part of our ambiguous Judaism, I spent the first few years of elementary school in Yeshiva, the Jewish equivalent of a Catholic school. Our days were long and split between religious training in the morning and secular school in the afternoon. In this setting, my first great life conflict exploded.

In the Jewish religious teachings, the universe was created by God in seven days around 5700 years ago. When I walked the halls of the Natural History Museum, I looked at exhibits of dinosaurs that walked the Earth millions and millions of years ago. At the planetarium, I was told that the universe started in the big bang over ten billion years ago. My confusion grew, turmoil arose, and I lashed out. I stood up in my Torah class and called our teacher, a rabbi, a liar. Obviously, my intellectual side matured way before my political smarts. I was promptly expelled and tossed out into the cold, hard, secular world, landing in Public School 216 in Brooklyn, New York.

In my own tiny way I had fallen into the gray and confusing space between faith and science.

I recovered from the shame of the expulsion. My parents forgave me. God forgave me. I had chosen science, but I still had many questions about God, creation, life, the universe, and everything.

These were life-molding factors that made me, me. After high school, my educational path took me to one of the city colleges, and finally to a PhD in theoretical physics. My experiences as a child of Holocaust survivors, a precocious and bright child, an inquisitive student, and a serious scientist led me to the very place that I noted in the opening paragraphs of this chapter.

How is it possible that we know so much about such complex systems as the universe and life? Is there a God? How do reason and faith coexist and even act in a mutually supportive way? What is my role in the universe and my relationship to God, assuming that he does exist?

The results of my quest were both powerful and surprising.

I present this work, neither as a book of science nor as a book of theology, but as something else entirely. Rather, this book is a detailed account of one person's faith journey, a mission to align faith and science within the mind of a child, becoming a man, becoming a scientist. The insights and knowledge learned along the way have led me to the present. Today, I am a compendium of all this curiosity and analysis. I hope sharing these ideas has value to you, the reader, and to me, the author.

Twenty-two years ago, after the birth of my daughter and fourth child, I converted to Christianity, becoming a Presbyterian and joining a thriving church in Kingwood, Texas. I enjoyed deep and probing chats with our minister and was asked to give a series of talks to the Adult Sunday school on my faith journey. The talks were titled "A Quantum Leap of Faith." After the first class something magical happened. Attendance went from barely filling a small classroom to overflowing in one week. By the third week we were in the sanctuary. What I quickly discovered was that my ideas were resonating in our well-educated congregation, and that many people were struggling to balance a church view of the world with a real worldview. I was trying to answer questions that everyone around me struggled with, as well.

When I gave the series a second time in Kingwood, we also invited the congregation of the First Presbyterian Church in Houston which was filled with doctors from the medical center, professors from Rice University, and even astronauts. Once again the response was overwhelming.

People were excited, inspired, and moved by my efforts to unify reasoning and faith. Many came to me and said that I should write the class material as a book. Life intervened. I was too busy to get to it then but I promised that I would do it someday when things slowed down. They never did.

Sixteen years ago, we moved to Ann Arbor, Michigan. One of my dearest friends is very active in one of the local Presbyterian churches, and the subject of these talks came up in one of our conversations. Before I knew it, I had volunteered and dusted off my old notes and presented the series to a new group in a new setting.

The same magic happened.

Clearly there were important ideas in this work.

To those of you who are just picking up this book—enjoy. Open your minds and fasten your seatbelts. Headgear is optional.

And of course, thank you, God, for making me, me, and for any wisdom that I might pass along by these musings. I have been truly blessed.

I invite you to embark upon this complex journey with me. As you grapple with these great questions and derive answers based on both faith and science, you will be attempting to bring the two worldviews together in a satisfying intellectual and spiritual way. You will realize how structured and methodical the intellectual development of scientists has been. You will be looking at the great mystery that is life, the miraculous power of the mind, the history of the universe, the world as depicted in Genesis and in the sciences, the almost metaphysical directions gleaned from cosmology, relativity, quantum mechanics, and string theory, and finally into the very nature of the soul. The answers will lead you to new questions. This is a good thing, since questioning is what we humans do best.

You also will realize that many of the greatest scientific minds have looked into the answers to the very same questions repeatedly. For example, Einstein and Hawking often considered concepts involving the mind of God and God's role in the creation of the universe. The widely held belief that scientists are godless atheists is flawed. The actual concepts and questions they have developed in the arena of theology are quite profound and important.

It is with this thought that we start our journey.

The Mystery That Is Life

> To the honest man...the origin of life appears...
> to be almost a miracle, so many are the conditions
> which would have to be satisfied to get it going.
>
> —Francis Crick, biochemist, discoverer of the
> structure of the DNA molecule

What, exactly, is life?

The Earth teems with it. Everywhere we look, even in the most extreme environments, life thrives. It fills every ecological niche on our planet. We have found organisms thriving near volcanic vents on the floor of the ocean, far from the sun and air that we consider necessary for life. Our planet has had several major catastrophic events that have wiped out almost all life on our planet and yet, from the few forms that survived, life has proliferated again throughout the world.

Life.

Tenacious. Tough. Resilient. Brilliantly capable of exploiting whatever environmental changes are thrown at it. A great miracle.

But what is it?

Scientists and philosophers have searched for a good definition for almost as long as there has been organized thought. Here is a good scientific definition:

"Living organisms are autopoietic systems: self-constructing, self-maintaining, energy-transducing, autocatalytic entities" in which information needed to construct the next generation of organisms is stabilized in nucleic acids that replicate within the context of whole cells and work with other developmental resources during the life cycles of organisms, but they are also "systems capable of evolving by variation and natural selection: self-reproducing entities, whose forms and functions are adapted to their environment and reflect the composition and history of an ecosystem" (Harold, F. M. 2001. *The Way of the Cell: Molecules, Organisms and the Order of Life*. New York: Oxford University Press).

Defining a few terms may help:

Autopoiesis. It literally means "whose seed is in itself," or a "process whereby a system produces its own organization and maintains and constitutes itself in a space (e.g., a biological cell, a living organism)."

Quite a trick! Yet every living thing in the universe has this property. Self-maintaining. Life boldly defies the law of thermodynamics (Entropy), while every other chemical and physical system in the universe is a slave to them, which is interesting in itself, if not miraculous.

Nonliving systems are *entropic*. As time passes they become more chaotic and disordered that leads into states of increasing entropy and disorder. Life is *anti-entropic*. That means it maintains structure and order and flushes its entropic chaos to the world around it. Life gives off heat, wastes, and other by-products into its surroundings. The order preserved in the living system is more than paid for by the disorder it expels. Living systems have a special dispensation from chaos. Once they die, the former living thing succumbs to thermodynamics and begins to decay into chaotic nonliving components.

We understand that living systems are made of the same raw physical and chemical components as nonliving things. The chemistries can be measured, analyzed, and even manipulated. Knowing this complex integration of information has empowered the human mind with incredible, almost miraculous, capabilities such as the treatment of disease. Someday that may lead us to a cure for aging and death.

What is life?

What else distinguishes a living thing from a dead thing?

Philosophers have struggled with this question since the days of ancient Greece. How does a collection of chemicals not very different from plain dirt start as a tiny egg and grow into something so much more complex than a tree?

Even more profound, how does consciousness arise in a living thing? At the moment of death, exactly what changes the state of a living system to nonliving? Believe it or not, the boundary between life and death is not scientifically precise, which has given rise to massive turf and ethical wars in modern medicine.

We are not able to define life simply, or even death for that matter.

Interesting, isn't it?

And, of course, there is the big question: How did life arise?

I remember learning about the origin of life in school. I was taught that life arose in the early seas of the Earth as a result of a random process over billions of years. Indeed, the concept of evolution is at the root of our biological understanding of everything.

Try to picture it. Life on the Earth arose around 3.8 billion years ago, less than a hundred million years after the oceans formed. The idea that life simply happened as a result of random mixing of organic chemicals has always bothered me. One hundred million years just does not seem long enough. Scientific research has shown us that life requires innumerable complex structures and processes to operate.

They have struggled with the idea that random mixing of chemicals alone could give rise to a system that requires a number of fully developed interdependent subassemblies to work. Even if random processes would work, wouldn't they need trillions of years to try all the combinations?

There is a mystery here.

As I googled the origin of life, I came across a cute analogy that mirrors my misgivings. The story theorizes how handheld calculators might have arisen using the same random mixing mechanism.

> "The origin of Handheld Calculators: Let's put the current paradigm of how life on Earth might have begun in terms of the computer analogy. The fossil record indicates that there were handheld calculators with 240 kilobytes of stored programs—prokaryotic cells—in existence almost as soon as the earth cooled. Here is how the story might go:
>
> Handheld calculators originated when special conditions allowed the formation of silicon chips and circuit boards (primitive genes). Heat, possibly generated by radioactivity, volcanic activity, or the impact of a meteor, melted some sand to form a silicon flake. Random splashing of molten metal caused metal filaments to form a circuit board on the flake. Lightning provided the first source of electrical power. This primitive proto-calculator somehow acquired ten to 25 bytes of stored programs (40 to 100 nucleotides) that enabled it to

have some function that made it useful. Batteries (allowing independent metabolism) came later. The first batteries were iron acid batteries, formed in mud pockets. Lithium batteries were a very late development. Now we find evidence for only the fully evolved handheld calculators similar to the ones used today, with function keys and lengthy stored programs, because the fossil record is incomplete.

Silly isn't it? When we look at the miraculous construct of deoxyribonucleic acid (DNA) and the incredible complexity of its functionality, the mystery is even more profound. Chemistry shows us that DNA needs enzymes and enzymes need DNA. How could one have been created without the other? Which came first—the chicken or the egg?

**DNA—My Favorite Chemical Structure in the Universe
(Some of my best friends are made from DNA!)**

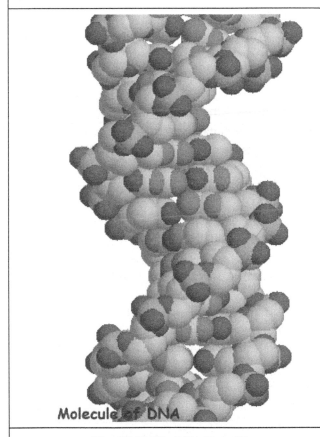

Molecule of DNA

The RNA World by Brig Klyce

MICHAEL SIMON BODNER, PH.D.

Virtually all biologists now agree that bacterial cells cannot form from nonliving chemicals in one step. If life arises from nonliving chemicals, there must be intermediate forms, precellular life.

The step from prelife to life is really a quantum leap of its own. Biologists will spend the next few decades trying to bridge the gaps, looking for an understandable mechanism to explain how the transition from precellular to early cellular life occurred. One possible candidate is ribonucleic acid (RNA), which is capable of acting somewhat like genes and enzymes on its own. *All* that is left to discover are the intermediate steps (and artifacts).

Even if we assume that the bridging process from prelife to life does exist, we are still left with the problem of inadequate time. As we noted earlier, life arose in the seas less than a hundred million years after the seas formed.

> The only premise that all of the precellular theories share is that it would be an extremely long time before the first bacterial cells evolved. If precellular life somehow got going, it could then conceivably begin to crank out, by some precellular process, random strings of nucleotides and amino acids, trying to luck into a gene or a protein with advantages which would lead to bacterial life. There is no evidence in life today of anything that produces huge quantities of new, random strings of nucleotides or amino acids, some of which are advantageous. But if

30

precellular life did that, it would need lots of time to create any useful genes or proteins. How long would it need? After making some helpful assumptions we can get the ratio of actual, useful proteins to all possible random proteins up to something like one in 10^{500} (ten to the 500th power). So it would take, barring incredible luck, something like 10^{500} trials to probably find one. Imagine that every cubic quarter-inch of ocean in the world contains ten billion precellular ribosomes. Imagine that each ribosome produces proteins at ten trials per minute (about the speed that a working ribosome in a bacterial cell manufactures proteins). Even then, it would take about 10^{450} years to probably make one useful protein. But Earth was formed only about 4.6×10^{9} years ago. The amount of time available for this hypothetical protein creation process was maybe a hundred million or 10^{8} years. And now, to make a cell, we need not just one protein, but a minimum of several hundred.

Therefore, even if we allow precellular life, there is a problem getting from there to proteins, genes and cells. The random production of proteins does not succeed as an explanation. Other intermediate, unspecified stages must be imagined. We could call these stages post-precellular life. By whatever means, life's evolution through these stages would have to be time-consuming.

Clive Trotman, in his book, *The Feathered Onion: The Creation of Life in the Universe*, echoes a great many biologists and biochemists who think there has not been enough time for random processes to create systems even as complex as the earliest life on our planet.

> Traces of the earliest forms of life on Earth reveal that they were already highly complex, consisting of cells, genes, proteins and an intricate metabolism. Life at the biochemical level was in many ways as complex in those early organisms as it is today, which leaves us with a massive gap in our knowledge about how life got started in a relatively short space of time. We know that evolution takes million of years to complete even small changes in animals and plants. Can we really accept that the transition from simple chemicals to primitive yet complex life forms occurred in such a short time-span?

In the early 1950s Stanley L. Miller, working in the laboratory of Harold C. Urey at the University of Chicago, conducted the first experiment designed to clarify the chemical reactions that occurred on the primitive earth. In a lab, he created an "ocean" of water, which he heated, forcing water vapor to circulate through the apparatus. The flask at the top contained an "atmosphere" consisting of methane (CH_4), ammonia (NH_3), hydrogen (H_2), and the circulating water vapor. Next, he exposed the gases to a continuous electrical discharge (lightning), causing the gases to interact. Water-soluble products of those reactions then passed through a condenser and dissolved in the mock ocean. The experiment yielded many amino acids and enabled Miller to explain how they had formed. For instance, glycine appeared after reactions in the atmosphere produced simple compounds, formaldehyde and hydrogen cyanide, that participated in the set of reactions shown below.

Years later, a meteorite that struck near Murchison, Australia, that contained a number of the same amino acids that Miller had identified and in roughly the same relative amounts. Such coincidences lent credence to the idea that Miller's protocol approximated the chemistry of the prebiotic earth.

> "To go from a bacterium to people is less of a step than to go from a mixture of amino acids to a bacterium." Lynn Margulis interviewed in *The End of Science*, by John Horgan. Addison-Wesley Publishing Company, Inc., 1996, 140–141.

This experiment led to two conclusions: that the organic chemicals necessary for life arise naturally during planetary synthesis on an Earthlike planet, and that these chemicals exist in space as well. Subsequent astronomical observations have measured organic chemicals and even amino acids in gas clouds throughout the galaxy.

One of the most logical solutions to the time problem comes from the synthesis of Miller's experimental results and the extraterrestrial observations. Crick himself proposed that life (RNA) must have originated in space, and that the early oceans were "seeded" by molecules in meteorites born upon the solar wind. This theory is called panspermia:

"The theory that microorganisms or biochemical compounds from outer space are responsible for originating life on Earth and possibly in other parts of the universe where suitable atmospheric conditions exist."

A number of scientists have come to see this as a real alternative to the random slope model, which opens the discussion to the origin of life in the universe.

How does all this sit with the theological beliefs concerning the origins of life? When we talked about Genesis, we proposed that the Bible does in fact discuss a phased, periodic, process for the creation of the universe, the solar system, the Earth, and life itself. The actual language is,

"And God said, Let the earth bring forth grass, the herb yielding seed, and the fruit tree yielding fruit after his kind, whose seed is in itself, upon the earth: and it was so" (King James Bible "Authorized Version," Cambridge Edition).

Look at the concepts embedded here. "Let the Earth bring forth," plant life, seeds, "fruit tree yielding fruit after his kind." The concept of *species* is right there in Genesis, as is the idea that life is autopoietic—"whose seed is in itself."

Wow!

The Earth brought forth life from its fundamental components. The chemicals that make up all life in the universe are primarily carbon, oxygen, hydrogen, and nitrogen. COHN exists in the universe, even in the heavens.

The potential for the bringing forth of life is "wired" into the stellar and planetary evolution schema.

Life happens.

Life Evolves

Not only does life happen, but also it has re-happened several times on our own home planet. Scientists believe that life returned after several sterilization catastrophes in our early history. Massive comets and asteroids continued to strike the Earth with great velocity even after life arose. Each of these violent events wiped out a huge percentage of early life. Most scientists (and much of the general population) believe that the dinosaurs were wiped out by such an event about sixty-five million years ago.

Once these cosmic catastrophes became less frequent, life had time to bloom. And bloom it did. The remaining life systems spread and adapted to fill the empty niches formerly occupied by the great reptiles.

There have been many mass extinctions in Earth's history. The *Columbia Encyclopedia, Sixth Edition* (2001) offers the following detail:

> Mass extinction:
>
> The extinction of a large percentage of the earth's species, opening ecological niches for other species to fill. There have been at least ten such events. The five greatest were those of the final Ordovician period (approximately 435 million years ago), the late Devonian period (357 million years ago), the final Permian period (250 million years ago), the late Triassic period (198 million years ago), and the final Cretaceous period (65 million years ago). The most devastating was that at the end of the Permian period, when an estimated 95% of marine species and eight of 27 insect orders were lost. The best-known mass extinction is that at the end of the Cretaceous period, when the dinosaurs and many other plants and animals disappeared and up to 75% of all marine genera were lost. The most recent mass extinction was that of the late Eocene epoch, approximately 54 million years ago.

Life not only happens but also it reemerges in new forms each time it is wiped out. It adapts to an incredibly complex set of changing conditions and thrives. It evolves and fills all available ecological niches.

There, I've said it. Life evolves.

One of the most contentious boundaries between science and theology is the debate over Darwin's theory of evolution. This battle focuses on some fundamental issues that are not even close to the real wonder of what is going on. As we have shown, the universe evolves. All the elements other than hydrogen arose by complex stellar processes after the creation! Stars, galaxies, and planets came into being by following the rules formulated by the laws of physics at the moment after the big bang.

Planets formed—utilizing discrete processes that follow scientific rules—and developed atmospheres and seas and the chemical building blocks of life.

Life not only arose but also is capable of doing something miraculous. It is able to adapt to almost any condition that is thrown against it. It has shown its tenacity and diversity throughout the present world and in history. Each time the conditions on Earth catastrophically alter, almost wiping out all life, life has the potential to rebound. When the dinosaurs were wiped out, their DNA-based cousins exploded with new adaptations into new species capable of exploiting the niches vacated by the extinct species.

Miraculous!

The current battle between the evolutionists and creationists is leveraged around the concept of intelligent design (ID), in which the creationists are trying to merge science and theology.

"The movement's (Intelligent Design) main positive claim is that there are things in the world, most notably life, that cannot be accounted for by known natural causes and show features that, in any other context, we would attribute to intelligence. Living organisms are too complex to be explained by any natural—or, more precisely, by any mindless—process. Instead, the design inherent in organisms can be accounted for only by invoking a designer, and one who is very, very smart" (H. Allen Orr, The New Yorker, 2005-05-30).

Darwinians believe that all the diversity in living things arises from random mutations and natural selection, whereas ID sees it as a part of a fixed plan. While I acknowledge the power implied in the design of life, my vote for the process goes to Darwinism. In our own natural history, we have seen massive upheavals and climactic catastrophes. As discussed earlier, life persevered through, literally, Earth-shattering events.

The actual plan for the continuation of life is simple. If things change, like the plants upon which an animal feeds being wiped out by a change in the weather (for a long time), the numbers of these animals drop due to starvation and then lack of procreation. If at this time there is another animal that can better survive the change, say by eating cactus in a drought, it will grow in number and fill the area vacated by the starving leaf eaters. Even when comet strikes lead to thousands of years without sunshine (due to dust—

the nuclear winter model), some forms of life responded to the stress and thrived. Mutations that gave offspring some advantage over its progenitors led to success for the new variation and, often, extinction for the less-efficient cousins. It makes sense. The survival of the fittest makes sense in biology as it does in business and economics.

Evolution works. Darwin's theory is sound and easy to document. Fossils and chemistry support the central hypothesis for the mechanism of evolution. Genetics and DNA genome mappings show that life shares common roots, similar structures, and common processes.

The problem with ID is that it ignores the randomness of the universe. At its root it proposes that God (the Creator) designed the universe in such a way that it would give rise to us under automatic pilot. The probabilities that run from quantum mechanics on the microscopic scale to cosmic collisions like the asteroid causing the dinosaurs' extinction make it unthinkable that a linear plan or design would get to a specific endpoint. What if the Dinousaur Extinction Asteroid (DEA) had missed the Earth altogether? Dinosaurs ruled the plant for hundreds of millions of years prior to the event and most probably would have thrived and diversified over the last sixty-five million. Mammals would not have found empty niches, and our species might not have ever evolved. How then could there have been a plan to make man?

And does ID believe that man is the ultimate life-form? What is there to prevent evolution from continuing to *improve* our design? Might not our descendents develop longer and more dexterous thumbs after thousands of years of texting on cell phones and playing video games? If global warming really does flood most of the world, who is to say that man might develop gills and return to the sea?

What will humanity look like a million or so years from now?

The universe in which we live is the result of a nearly infinite set of decision points that have led to the here and now. We exist because all the things that were necessary for our existence happened. My mother and father met, fell in love, married, moved to New York, and had me. If either of my parents had died in a concentration camp, or not gone back to Poland after liberation, I would not exist.

We are here because we are here.

The species that survived and thrived did so because the conditions were such that they were able to do so.

There is a place for an intelligent designer here, but my definition is much broader. God designed the universe in such a way so that, via consistent natural laws and processes, life arose and evolved to meet whatever conditions were thrown at it! Think of it—every time life was challenged on our planet, it adapted. The process of change was built into the assembly itself. Rather than having a fixed design, life is a system that can change as needed, improve (or go extinct) in response to external conditions.

When one synthesizes the concepts of quantum mechanics and *multiple realities*, as we will discuss in coming chapters, one realizes that there is a reality that corresponds to each possible outcome of every decision point in history. The reality in which we live seems perfect for life as we know it because we live here. This is our reality. All the realities in which cosmic collisions and random mutations wound up not leading to us are realities in which we do not exist!

The number of permutations leading to us biologically are not limited to this reality, but rather have worked themselves out in unseen other time lines.

It bears repeating: We are here because we are here.

The reality in which we live seems as perfect for life as we know it because we live here. This is our reality. Otherwise, all the cosmic collisions and random mutations would have led to realities in which we do not exist! In time lines where DNA did not arise, we, and all life on Earth, did not arise. Those realities are not ours. This one is.

The Creator set up the universe in such a way that human beings were *possible*, not *predetermined*. The Creation is still awe-inspiring and profound. The Creator has demonstrated even more intelligence than credited to Him by the ID community.

We are products of Creation, and yet our minds have created mathematics and science and led us to understand the chain of events that led to us being here at all. R. J. C. Wilding discusses the work of another one of the great minds:

Just after the turn of the century, D'Arcy Thompson wrote On Growth and Form (revised and reprinted in 1942). His attention was drawn to the unity of life and the relationship between form and function. His many drawings not only reflect his love of nature, he was diverted by shellfish, frogs, snowflakes and bubbles, but his drawings also reveal a perception for mathematical pattern and mechanical design which were well ahead of his time. It is just as well he was not dependent on the approval of a committee for his research funds, as he would surely have had all his proposals turned down. Firstly, because there were too many of them, and secondly, because his work is quite free of statistical analysis, an icon of modern science. His genius lay in making order out of the great diversity he recorded. All his observations seem to have been collected for the contribution they could make to his search for a unifying design in nature. He was looking for something that would tie all the repeated biological phrases together, a unity of purpose amongst all the diversity. And he found it, in mathematical expressions for the helix of a shell or the shapes of growing cells; he found it in the structure of snow flakes, the cracks in basalt and the stripes of a zebra.

He argued that there were common laws at work.

The search for differences or fundamental contrasts between the phenomena of organic and inorganic, of animate and inanimate things, has occupied many scientists, while the search for commonality of principle or essential similarities has been pursued by few; the contrasts are apt to loom too large, great though they be."

DOES OTHER LIFE EXIST IN THE COSMOS?

The fact that life evolves and endures by adapting to changes is a powerful testament to the effectiveness and power of its design. Why would God create life for a single set of conditions at a single time in the history of an ecosystem as dynamic and complex as Earth?

Consider the profound implications. If the potential for life is natural and can occur given the right conditions, it probably has arisen in a great many places across the cosmos. Even the concept of right conditions has expanded to encompass extreme environments. Just as we have seen the voracious tendency for life to adapt in extreme conditions on our own planet, we must accept that this tendency is universal. With literally billions and billions of star systems with the same chemistry and physics as our own, life is probably everywhere.

The possibilities are endless. Even if the conditions seem inhospitable or toxic to life as we know it, we can expect to find life on Mars and on the moons of the gas giants (Saturn and Jupiter).

Mars has captured our focus for centuries as having potential for life. It is of similar size and construction as the Earth, with "ice caps" at its poles, and enough of an atmosphere to drive sandstorms visible from Earth even by amateur astronomers. When early astronomers thought they saw canals on the Martian surface, imaginations went wild. H. G. Wells formulated a seminal story in *War of the Worlds* about hostile alien life and our vulnerability. The story had such power that people actually believed and reacted to Orson Welles famous radio broadcast of the *Invasion from Mars*.

The terms "Martians" and "aliens" became interchangeable in our imagination, and they were always bad news. Hollywood and the science fiction writers have leveraged our fear of the unknown to sell lots of movies and books. Indeed, *E.T.* in 1982 and *Close Encounters of the Third Kind* in 1977 were the first films to propose benevolent alien life.

When we sent probes to Mars to look for life, they sent back pictures showing evidence that water once flowed freely on the surface of Mars. The eerie landscapes looked like the high deserts on Earth.

**An image of Mars from the
Viking II Lander**

The Viking Lander in 1976 conducted a great experiment. We concocted a "cosmic chicken soup," a really delicious feast for any red-blooded Martian (forgive the pun). The glucose nutrient had at the end of its molecule a radioactive carbon atom. The idea was to scoop up a handful of Martian sand and dump it into the soup. A life-form would metabolize the soup and release carbon dioxide gas with a radioactive carbon atom. This gas would go into a second chamber and be detected by a Geiger counter. When the experiment was run, the radiation detector found radioactive carbon dioxide pouring into the second chamber. Phase one thus signaled the detection of life on Mars.

Phase two involved taking the sample and incinerating it. In the flames, the probe looked for spectra indicating the presence of DNA-organic material. None was found. The great controversy began: what ate the soup?

Now, almost thirty years later, scientists are revisiting the data and attempting an analysis based on different assumptions. What if the sensitivity of the spectral analysis had been too low? Was there too little organic material to show up on the spectral life detection unit? What if our definition of life had been too narrow to encompass different life-forms?

As an aside, I have always felt that conducting this experiment on another planet had been quite rude. Imagine that a robot probe from another planet landed in New York City. A door opens and a few people enter. They are fed a fabulous lunch. And while happily digesting their meal, they are incinerated for analysis. Hardly a polite first contact!

Seriously, the quest for life on Mars will continue. New and better experiments will be conducted. While the evidence for extraterrestrial life is tantalizing, the proof needs to be irrefutable.

When the Cassini-Huygens spacecraft landed on Saturn's moon Titan, it found a sea of liquid methane and a crust with the consistency of crème brûlée. There, methane chilled to a liquid state by the unimaginable cold of the distant moon assumed the role taken by water on Earth.

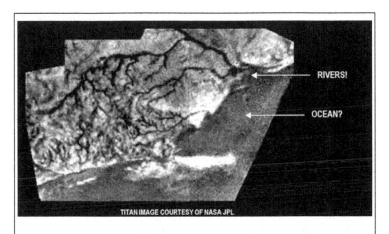

TITAN IMAGE COURTESY OF NASA JPL

Images sent back from Titan by Huygens show river channels and deltas carved by methane rain.

Everything needed for life is there: organic chemistry; a liquid sea, and heat from volcanic or radioactive strata. Life could have arisen there. But what kind of life would it be?

Indeed what kinds of life are possible? Life-forms on Earth are carbon based using oxygen/CO_2 for respiration and a COHN metabolism, but this chemistry would never work on Titan, or on a billion undiscovered worlds. The range of possibilities explodes to the infinite.

Does life exist elsewhere in the universe? Most scientists will answer with a resounding yes. Do they look like humans with bumps on their foreheads or green skin? Probably not. The reason alien species in *Star Trek* and most sci-fi movies look like us and speak English has more to do with Hollywood make believe than any logic.

Then what might alien life look like? The range is literally unimaginable. Consider the range of diversity on Earth and multiply it exponentially. There could be life based on silicon and other atoms structurally similar to carbon.

When we get to Mars (or Titan), will we even be able to identify life? We have ways to go to broaden our understanding and definitions, but I for one can hardly wait for the chance.

Finding life on another planet in our solar system would have a profound and deep impact on our society and psyches, opening the door for more intense philosophical and theological questions. If the panspermia theory is correct, we might even find RNA or DNA on local planets. No one knows.

Is it reasonable to think we are the only form of advanced and intelligent life in such a vast universe? As Carl Sagan says in *Contact*, "Seems like an awfully big waste of space."

Why haven't we found life?

This is an easy question to answer.

The universe is big!

Very big!

When measured against the size of the universe, our current technology severely limits our speed of space travel. The closest star systems with planets are three to ten light-years from Earth. A light-year is the distance that light travels in a year. Since light moves at 186,000 miles per second, these distances are difficult to conquer. Our fastest space rockets travel at 25,000 miles per hour, which translates to an almost immeasurable fraction of the speed of light. It would take our astronauts hundreds of years to reach even the nearest star.

The only way to sustain such a long trip would be building giant colony ships that could carry hundreds of passengers and keep them and their subsequent generations intact for centuries. Many science fiction stories have employed this model with all its benefits and pitfalls. Even if the travelers were convinced, they would find a life-bearing planet at the end of the trip. This would be a tough journey.

This same distance and time problem would confront all civilizations in the universe capable of space travel. The trips would be so long, expensive, and dangerous that most intelligent races would not even try.

A second school of thought allows the possibility of building extremely powerful rockets that could travel at near light speeds. Since time slows down for astronauts traveling at these speeds, this would add the magic of the special theory of relativity to the mix. As measured by people on Earth, the several hundred years of the trip would take only a few months. Better, but even if they found nothing, turned around and returned to Earth, hundreds and hundreds of years would have passed. They would have experienced a journey of a lifetime, but everyone on Earth would be long dead by the time of their return.

The fact that time expands would almost negate the possibility of any continuity for both civilizations. Imagine if the Starship Enterprise got an emergency call, like needing a vaccine to combat a vicious plague at Starbase 12 a mere hundred light-years away. If the ship uses impulse engines to go at 99.999% of light speed, they could make the trip in ten minutes. Nonetheless, it would arrive at Starbase 12 one hundred years later from the colonists' viewpoint. Everyone would be dead from the plague for nearly a century. The dispirited crew would travel back to Earth and arrive two hundred years after they left, where no one would remember who they were or why they had left.

This would be a rotten way to run a federation of planets, so the writers of Star Trek and Star Wars and just about every other space adventure needed to come up with a mechanism to overcome the distance issues and the limitations of relativity. The enterprise had the capability to move at warp speed (exponentially faster than light) in order to bypass the effects of time dilation. They also needed a subspace radio system to talk to people across the galaxy in real time. Unless we discover the physics behind warp drive or hyperspace and figure out how to do instant messaging across the cosmos, we will be stuck in our local space forever.

Since we do not have (faster than light) FTL technology and have not yet discovered subspace radios, we are left with only way to seek out new civilizations. In a worldwide effort known as (Search for Extraterrestrial Intelligence) SETI, we scan the skies with radio telescopes looking for intelligent signals from out there in space.

Less than a hundred years ago, SETI began looking for candidate signals. If one is found, scientists believe we could extract the information and thus prove the existence of an extraterrestrial intelligence.

Let's say that tonight we find such a signal from a source thirty light-years away. We decipher a language (probably mathematics based) and send a greeting.

We say, "Hello from Earth."

Thirty years from now, the message is received by our newly found friends. They decipher it and send back a response: "Hello. How are you doing?"

Sixty years from now we get their answer and fire back, "Great, and you?"

This doesn't seem to be a very lively conversation, but such are the limits of signals passing between us at finite (although very fast) speeds.

SETI will probably work only to identify intelligent sources, but will be unable to grant us communication capabilities when the discovery is made.

That said, Carl Sagan in his wonderful book and movie, *Contact*, came up with an entertaining (and quite plausible) set of solutions to the constraints of time and distance. In the movie, the astrophysicists find a SETI signal with non-prime number sequences. Upon examining this unnatural signal, they discover the format of an early television frame. Once decoded, they see pictures of Adolph Hitler opening the 1936 Olympics in Berlin, one of the first television broadcasts on Earth. Since the signal is coming from far enough away for the round-trip of the signal, they realize that our alien friends were very clever and sent back our own signal to say, "We got it and are capable of understanding the mathematics to decipher this image."

Subsequently, the scientists discover that the pictures contain another data stream, which turns out to be plans for building a wormhole machine that would allow someone to traverse the great distances across space by passing through another dimension. The wormholes turn out to be the intergalactic subway system that enables intelligent civilizations to cross space without the problems we have discussed.

Until we actually figure out how to build wormhole machines or warp drives or talk on subspace radios, we will continue our lonely existence here on Earth and speculate about intelligent life in the universe.

Many people find it odd that we have not found any radio transmissions from advanced civilizations. After all, the universe is not only big but also it is old. There should be millions of civilizations even more advanced than we are. Why is the spectrum so quiet?

Several scientists and philosophers have posed that perhaps civilizations reach a point in their technological development when they achieve the capability to destroy themselves, either in cataclysmic wars or through bio/ecological accidents. Does the lack of signals mean that civilizations out there have not made it past this dangerous phase in their development?

If each civilization rises, develops technological power beyond their limits to control it, and then dies, this offers a depressing view of the fate of intelligent life in the universe. In the New Testament, Revelations paints a picture of a horrible war between the forces of good and evil in the end of days. To some, the ultimate outcome of civilizations that derive power from knowledge without sufficient ethical and moral foundations is total and final annihilation. Interesting how biblical parables can wrap around even cosmic hypothesis.

Does the Bible preclude the existence of other beings in the universe? Considering the scale of the universe and the potential for there being billions and billions of civilizations, I find it unreasonable to assume that God only cares about us.

If we get to Alpha Centauri someday, will we find that its inhabitants are religious? Would the aliens worship the same God? Would they have the same ethical and moral foundations, perhaps the same conceptual Ten Commandments? Would each civilization be visited by the Son of God?

It is certainly within God's ability to manage billions and billions of peoples. As to whether He loves us the most, have you ever asked your parents if they love you more than your siblings? I believe that there is life throughout the universe and that the Creator is also their God.

The next time you are far from the city lights on a clear, cold, moonless night, look up at the stars. As you look at all stars in the sky, think about the creation the Creator, and the possibility of billions of God's creatures looking back at you.

You will be humbled by God's magnificence and awesome power that is before your eyes.

The Mind of the Child,
the Mind of the Physicist,
and the Mind of God

How do our minds make sense of the universe? Some answers may be found by examining three important viewpoints: the mind of the child, the mind of the physicist, and the mind of God. We have personal knowledge of the first two, and the third is beyond our grasp. The emergence of the mind involves two distinct developmental processes: our initial effort to understand our surroundings happens only once for every person on earth and this knowledge gained by all adults throughout human history leads to the communal mind of humankind in each generation.

To unlock the inscrutable mind of God, we can try to unpack the intellectual journey we all travel from being a child to becoming an adult. Observing children from birth to early school years exposes a set of amazing processes and events. Every mother and father holds their child's developmental process as a personal, intimate part of their parental workload. In trying to raise four children, I saw miraculous steps that appeared to be programmed at some core level. I watched their ability to sense their world, to respond to faces and sound, and to react to words long before they could talk. What parent could forget seeing their baby's first smile or hearing their first word?

Life in the world begins as newborns are whooshed from the womb, forced from a dark, warm, wet, and temperature-controlled environment into a world of bright lights and a scolding spank. Almost immediately after birth, some instinct kicks in that allow the baby to drink and eat. Imagine if they had to learn to suck on a nipple! Within minutes of birth, the baby has resolved this issue and moved on to responding to the warmth and cuddling that forgives the incredible shock of birth.

Healthy babies rapidly experience a myriad of new sounds, touch, tastes, and smells. They spend all their time observing and organizing the world around them. They reach out to touch and taste everything. They quickly become aware of what they like, what is comfortable and good, and what is bad. They learn to communicate displeasure or hunger or pain by crying. They quickly form predictable patterns of behavior. They smile and laugh and respond to others smiling and laughing at them.

Most amazingly babies soon learn to talk. By their first birthdays, they have a vocabulary of a few basic words. By their second birthday, they have vocabularies large enough to communicate most of their thoughts and needs. In a remarkably short time, they learn to control their bodies and walk upright. By three or four, they are truly little people, fully engaged in communication, capable of expressing complex thoughts and feelings.

It has always fascinated me how preschool children of all races and economic flavors function very much like scientists. They stack, pour, measure, mix, build, and disassemble objects as a regular part of play. They constantly experiment to see what would happen if they did this or that. This seems to be a key component of the mind of the child.

All children are scientists.

Jean Piaget, a well-respected philosopher and psychologist, was a pioneer in early child development. Over many years, he observed, interviewed, and studied the ways in which children perceived the world. His thesis was that children think and see the universe in a completely different way than adults from the moments of early speech. They exhibited a unique worldview based on a derived logic, trying to make sense of everything. Piaget saw children not as little blank slates with no order to their thoughts but as always applying their imagination to explain what they saw. Through this creative process, children developed logically consistent theories that satisfied their curiosity.

Children are not only scientists but also they are theoreticians!

Piaget's concepts of cognitive development were considered radical at the time because they crossed the boundaries between biology, psychology, and philosophy. He saw the root of all knowledge in the child's unique cognitive worldview, that the mind of the child lays the foundation for organizing knowledge in the adult mind.

> The essential functions of the mind consist in understanding and in inventing, in other words, in building up structures by structuring reality.
>
> —Piaget, J. (1971) *Science of Education and the Psychology of the Child*, New York: Viking Press

In other words, invention is a process through which a person creates a new view, models a new theory, and then submits that theory for testing.

This process begins when we are children. We make up theories and try to work things out in our own minds. This is very much like what our ancient predecessors did to organize their world. One could say that early mortals were driven by the mind of a child to create a workable worldview. Early religion met this exact need, as individuals observed the world and tried to answer questions about how it worked and why.

Piaget documented this theorizing process in children by recording many interviews. Here is one of classic experiment:

> Piaget: What makes the wind?
> Julia: The trees.
> P: How do you know?
> J: I saw them waving their arms.
> P: How does that make the wind?
> J (waving her hands): Like this. Only they are bigger. And there are lots of trees.
> P: What makes the wind on the ocean?
> J: It blows there from the land. No. It's the waves...

The fact that Julia's theory is incorrect is irrelevant. What is important is that she developed a coherent theory that was open to editing. *"No. it's the waves..."* And that she used her own mind and observational skills to arrive at this theory. As adults, we need to be careful not to dismiss young children's theories as *wrong* and immediately offer a dogmatic *final* answer. Children need to be allowed to reach a satisfying result based on their own cognitive process. To tell Julia why the wind *really* blows would not change her mind. The adult's answer lacks any structure and is thus doesn't make any sense to the child.

> Practicing the art of making theories may be more valuable for children than achieving meteorological orthodoxy; and if their theories are always greeted by 'Nice try, but this is how it really is...,' they might

give up after a while on making theories. As Piaget put it, 'Children have real understanding only of that which they invent themselves, and each time that we try to teach them something too quickly, we keep them from reinventing it themselves.' Disciples of Piaget have a tolerance for—indeed a fascination with—children's primitive laws of physics: that things disappear when they are out of sight; that the moon and the sun follow you around; that big things float and small things sink. Einstein was especially intrigued by Piaget's finding that seven-year-olds insist that going faster can take more time—perhaps because Einstein's own theories of relativity ran so contrary to common sense. (Seymour Papert, *Time Magazine*, March 29, 1999)

Based on Piaget's theories, we could postulate that a true physicist is actually an unspoiled child. Physicists build a series of internally satisfying theories that eventually form a consistent framework for explaining the universe. That's exactly what I did throughout my childhood. The mode of questioning and theorizing that helps a child organize the universe must be preserved for an adult to become a scientist.

Every child is, by his or her fundamental nature, a scientist. For most of them, the process of formal education manages to stifle their curiosity and wonder, turning them into (gasp!) normal adults. Indeed, Einstein himself had difficulty in school as a child.

> It is in fact nothing short of a miracle that the modern methods of instruction have not yet entirely strangled the holy curiosity of inquiry. (*The Quotable Einstein*, ed. Alice Calaprice, Princeton University Press, 1996)

Why is it that some of the world's best minds, who later in life become our most creative thinkers, often are not good at taking standardized tests? How can those who do poorly in school grow up to be great minds and create new thought and art? What part of the mind does school actually develop? Good questions. Several direct quotes may offer a window into their inner thoughts and feelings.

Brian Greene, author of *The Elegant Universe* and the NOVA PBS series, is widely considered to be one of the finest scientist and writer of his generation. He is often compared to Albert Einstein and Stephen Hawking, as well as Carl Sagan. Greene was asked why he chose physics as a career, and more specifically, why out of all subfields he chose string theory. His reply:

> Well, I think as an adolescent I had many of the questions and concerns that many adolescents do, you know—what's it all about, why are we here, what are we meant to be doing with our time and so forth. And it just occurred to me that many people

much smarter than I had thought of these questions through the ages and come up with various solutions, none of which I guess were completely satisfying, and it didn't seem to me that I was going to come up with a solution to those particular problems.

But it seemed to me that if one could gain a deep familiarity with the questions, a real profound understanding of the questions themselves—that is, why is there space, why is there time, why is there a Universe—then at least that would be the first step toward coming to answers. And physics is the field that has these questions as its real central motivating force behind the work that is done. So that was the main reason for physics.

Greene offers further illumination into the mind of the child/scientist in a dialogue with the renowned interviewer Robert Birnbaum:

> When I was a kid, my dad and I would walk down the street and the game was to look at some event that you might see—some of the examples I give in the book, some simple ones: somebody drops a coin, or an ant walking along some surface of some sort—and not describing the event from your point of view but describing the event from some arbitrary but definite point of view that is completely different from your own. From the point of view of the ant or the point of view of the falling coin, and so forth. And the challenge of the game was when

one or the other of us would give this description
of the world from this unspecified perspective to
go from the description to whose perspective it
was that things looked that way. If you are walking
along some brown cylindrical object and you have
these textured walls and there is this white stuff
coming from the sky—that would be the point of
view of an ant walking on a hot dog and you have
a street vendor putting sauerkraut on it. It's a very
interesting game in the sense of it allowed you to
see different perspectives, forced you constantly to
look at things from a very different point of view.

Reported in The Morning News, 26 February 2004,
www.themorningnews.org/archives/personalities/
birnbaum_v_brian_greene.php)

In a wonderful book, *Curious Minds: How a Child Becomes
a Scientist*, (ed. by John Brockman, Pantheon Books, 2004),
nearly thirty scientists talk about their childhood decisions
to become scientists and the events that influenced them.
Paul C. W. Davies, a professor of natural philosophy and
author of a number of delightful books (including *The
Mind of God*, Simon and Schuster, 1993), opens his essay:

I was born to be a theoretical physicist. I know it
sounds old fashioned, but there is such a thing as
a calling. And I had it—I still have it. From the
earliest age I can remember, I wanted to follow the
path I later chose when I eventually understood

what theoretical physics was and how professional science works. There was no epiphany. No key event precipitated my decision; no mentor inspired me.

He does go on to say: *"My family thought I was nuts."* Davies further muses:

There has always been something deep inside me—a sort of restlessness, verging on a sense of destiny—that drives me. It's a feeling of being drawn inexorably toward the serene heart of existence, a compulsion to search for hidden meaning in the universe, along with a conviction that meaning is in fact out there, lying just—but only just—within my grasp. But of course I am not alone in experiencing such intimations of cosmic significance, but most people outgrow them.

Shades of Piaget?

In another part of his essay, Davies relates a story about a dark-haired girl at school who interested him.

I contrived to sit opposite her one day, charged with the homework task of computing the trajectory of a ball projected up an inclined plane. As I was partway through several sheets of mathematics, the ravishing Lindsay looked across at me with a mixture of admiration and puzzlement. "What are you doing?" she asked. When I explained, she seemed completely mystified. "But how can you tell where a ball will go by writing squiggles on paper?"

Lindsay's question has haunted me ever since. How is it, indeed, that we can capture the workings of nature using human mathematics? I came to see the equations of theoretical physics as the hidden subtext of the universe. I realized how Galileo must have felt when he wrote that the book of nature is written in mathematical language. And I experienced something of the same thrill: the sense that nature itself was speaking to me, in code.

Indeed, Davies here expresses a wonder that all physicists share; that we *know* things, that we have uncovered the very language and process that drives creation. We have found the very "language of God"—mathematics. I often describe things in science as elegant, beautiful, or intricate. It sounds like I am describing art or music, which in fact I am. In the universe, creation is a work of art. It is simple and complex. What is most astounding is that we can understand it at all, that the complexity of the brain corresponds to the sheer complexity of the world.

The linkages between science and theology are not new. The Jewish scholar Maimonides once wrote:

Study astronomy and physics if you desire to comprehend the relation between the world and God's management of it. (Maimonides, the Guide for the Perplexed, Dover Publications, May, 2000)

Consider the beginnings of religion and theology and how the mind of the child develops into the mind of the adult. The emergence of observable, repeatable patterns in the world led to the creation of theories about how the universe worked and why. These theories involved gods and magic. Just as the theories of a child are not wrong, neither are the theories of early religion. The Nile really did flood each time a specific pattern presented itself in the night sky. The fact that the alignment of stars did not actually cause the flooding of the river is irrelevant. The theory served its believers well. It gave them guidance as to when to plant. Other signs from the gods told them when to reap and when to prepare for winter. Gods foretold of storms through signs in the sky and planets. Those who understood how to read the signs became priests and holy men and held high positions in society.

The theories worked. They were logically consistent. They provided satisfactory explanations that guided them. Theology served early civilizations well.

Yet the greatest mystery in the universe is the adult mind itself.

As I talked about earlier, when my children were born, I was awed at their development. I personally observed the cognitive stages of development that Piaget described. They began to organize the universe almost at birth. They developed communication and response to the environment in days. They developed complex neuromuscular capabilities like crawling and walking. Within twenty months, they developed speech and personalities and became little people. The time from the fertilization of the egg to the ability to walk, speak, and interact with the world is incredibly short. Even newborns display personalities. Children that share the same parents and developmental environments become unique individuals in their first few years.

Are there any real limits on the potential of a newborn? Healthy physical and emotional development proceeds in finely choreographed stages, leading to the emergence of individuals capable of all the greatness (and evil) of every person who has ever lived. But how much of what we are is programmed and how much is based from experience and environment?

We have learned a great deal about the mechanisms of matter, the laws of physics, and the nature of reality itself. Yet the workings of the human mind still elude us. If there is any place in our understanding for metaphysics, it will undoubtedly be in the realm of how we start from a single cell and grow into a being able to understand all of creation and questioning the existence and the motivations of the Creator Himself. This process is repeated everywhere on Earth thousands of times every day.

Where could you find a greater miracle?

The child becomes the adult, and after a bumpy period we call adolescence, many become scientists.

As scientists we discover the secrets of creation and seek out the ultimate mystery: the mind of God. While most people see science and theology as antithetical, I believe that as science expands to its edges, it often crosses over into the realms of religion.

Not surprisingly, we discover numerous quotes from the most brilliant minds addressing this crossover. Einstein offers:

> My religion consists of a humble admiration of the illimitable superior spirit who reveals himself in the slight details we are able to perceive with our frail and feeble mind. (http://www.quotationspage.com/quotes/Albert_Einstein)

When Einstein was asked about his belief in God, he answered, "Before God we are all equally wise—and equally foolish." About the relationship between science and religion, he said, "Science without Religion is lame, Religion without science is blind" (Albert Einstein, Science, Philosophy and Religion: A Symposium, 1941).

Stephen Hawking, arguably the most famous living voice of physics and cosmology, often talks about the mind of God and the nature of our ability to understand the universe. In 1989, in *Der Spiegel* he wrote: "We are just an advanced breed of monkeys on a minor planet of a very average star. But we can understand the Universe. That makes us something very special."

In his great book, *A Brief History of Time*, Hawking discusses the big bang and the beginning of time, space, and physics. He posed:

> Science seems to have uncovered a set of laws that, within the limits set by the uncertainty principle, tell us how the universe will develop with time, if we know its state at any one time. These laws may have originally been decreed by God, but it appears that he has since left the universe to evolve according to them and does not now intervene in it. But how did he choose the initial state or configuration of the universe? What were the "boundary conditions" at the beginning of time?
>
> One possible answer is to say that God chose the initial configuration of the universe for reasons that we cannot hope to understand. This would certainly have been within the power of an omnipotent being, but if he had started it off in such an incomprehensible way, why did he choose to let it evolve according to laws that we could understand? The whole history of science has been the gradual realization that events do not happen in an arbitrary manner, but that they reflect a certain underlying order, which may or may not be divinely inspired. It would be only natural to suppose that this order should apply not only to the laws, but also to the conditions at the boundary of space-time that specify the initial state of the universe. There may be a large number of models of the universe with

different initial conditions that all obey the laws. There ought to be some principle that picks out one initial state, and hence one model, to represent our universe.

This means that the initial state of the universe must have been very carefully chosen indeed if the hot big bang model was correct right back to the beginning of time. It would be very difficult to explain why the universe should have begun in just this way, except as the act of a God who intended to create beings like us.

Elsewhere in the book, Hawking addresses Einstein's question about the workings of the creation itself, "Einstein once asked the question, 'How much choice did God have in constructing the Universe?'"

Hawking responded, "If the no-boundary proposal is correct, He (God) had no freedom at all to choose the initial conditions."

Imagine the arrogance of such a statement! Yet the most remarkable aspect of this discourse is that human beings have delved deeply enough into the mystery of the origin of the universe that such an exchange is not arrogant. In the farthest realms of modern cosmology and physics, scientists are actually at the point of trying to understand the very ways the Creator worked and what was in His mind.

Breathtaking, isn't it?

The seeming arrogance of Hawking's statement needs to be mellowed by context. In the very last paragraph of *A Brief History of Time*, Hawking offers the following vision:

> However, if we discover a complete theory, it should in time be understandable by everyone, not just by a few scientists. Then we shall all, philosophers, scientists and just ordinary people, be able to take part in the discussion of the question of why it is that we and the universe exist. If we find the answer to that, it would be the ultimate triumph of human reason—for then we should know the mind of God.

Richard Feynman, another one of the great minds in physics in the twentieth century, proposes in his last book, *The Character of Physical Law* (Modern Library, 1994):

> Everything in physical science is a lot of protons, neutrons and electrons, while in daily life, we talk about men and history or beauty and hope. Which is nearer to God-beauty and hope or the fundamental laws? To stand at either end and to walk off that end of the pier only, hoping that out in that direction is a complete understanding, is a mistake.

It is at the intersection of these axes that we must probe. Truth is the exclusive realm neither of science nor of theology. They share the common goal of trying to understand many of the questions that the mind of the child can ask.

As a closing thought, let's go back to Hawking again: "Although science may solve the problem of how the universe began, it cannot answer the question: why does the universe bother to exist? Maybe only God can answer that."

I believe that this should be the goal of wisdom and reason—to continue the search for answers and explanations, to reach the *complete theory*, and, in time, to use the mind of the child/scientist to know the mind of God.

PHYSICS, COSMOLOGY, AND THE BIG BANG

The next two chapters lay the foundation for this book's premise. First, we will look at the *history of everything* as derived from science. In the next chapter, we will compare it to history as described in traditional theology. This comparison mirrors my own thought and faith journey. As travel companions, we will be able to construct a bridge spanning what is perceived as the great divide between science and religion.

In truth, humans have a very short history, spanning several thousands of years compared with the billions of years needed to prepare this one planet as a fit-dwelling place. Studying all our written and oral traditions underlies our knowledge about how we arrived at our current viewpoint. Everything else is derived from indirect observations and analysis. When we look at fossilized tree rings, for example, we can assume that variations in ring diameters a million years ago correspond to the trees cut down today. By examining these facts, we can formulate a climatological history of the world long before we were here. Using modern instrumentation and logic, we can look at the rocks of the Earth and out at the stars and galaxies and actually *know* what happened in the far past, not only before there were people but also even before there were stars and planets.

The history of everything according to science begins when early humans lived at a bare sustenance level, eking out an existence at the mercy of climates, predators, and diseases. Their ability to use tools, make and sustain fire, and grow food to supplement the hunt raised them to a niche just above the animals. The ability to speak and write allowed skills and learning to pass from generation to generation. Thus, each could move forward rather than starting from scratch. Early tools gave way to engineering, which led to the construction of roads and buildings. Farming methods and domesticated animals were able to sustain an ever-increasing population. Thus, early civilizations were more easily fed, clothed, and sheltered. This gave rise to entire classes of people with time to ponder and answer the questions raised by cave dwellers.

"Why am I here?"

"Where did we come from?"

"Where did the world come from?"

These great and pervasive questions arose in all cultures…and in the mind of every child. While individuals and family groups primarily focused on survival, civilized communities had time to ponder these questions.

Early thinkers made no distinction between theology and science, which served the same purpose using different methodologies. People observed cycles in nature, like sunrise, sunset, seasons, and tides. They were aware of life and death and creation and destruction. They recorded their observations and then created theories and hypotheses to explain them.

They realized that specific stars were in the same part of the sky each year when the weather changed.

Spring came.

The Nile flooded.

The ancients theorized that gods were responsible for these decipherable and predictable patterns. Science and theology both equally met our need to understand everything and feel safe in an ordered universe. It is from these early roots that religion, philosophy, and natural philosophy all grew together.

The mind of the child was in full bloom. The world became more ordered. Mathematics was discovered as a way to measure and track reality. Arithmetic and then geometry became the underpinnings of architecture and civil engineering, which developed and grew. Consider the profound accomplishments of the Egyptians, Greeks, and

Romans. We can only stand in awe that they constructed vast empires with roads, cities, and waterworks thousands of years before the development of modern knowledge and technology.

Using tools, writing, math, science, and theology, early civilizations achieved great heights through the power of the mind. How often do we look down on ancient biblical people by making a false temporal centric judgment that they were primitive? In thinking about the intellectual and creative power of the ancients, we should not dismiss their views as made by unsophisticated observers. Relegating all these stories to mythology and allegory merely reflects our own arrogance.

Yet modern academics and scientists dismiss even the possibility that some of their accounts might be accurate. In his powerful book, *Worlds in Collision*, Immanuel Velikovsky proposed that events in the Bible, such as the Flood and the destruction of Sodom and Gomorrah, were based on things that really happened! This claim sparked a great controversy.

Velikovsky was an extremely educated man with degrees in medicine and law. As a dedicated scholar and researcher, he attacked problems he perceived in the chronologies of the ancient world. He thought that ancient writings, both scriptural and secular, indicate that those civilizations were hit by several massive catastrophes. He extrapolated that actual astronomical events might explain many of the miraculous occurrences in the Old Testament and other writings from that time. Though Velikovsky was neither an astronomer nor a scientist, he dared to attribute scientific explanations to biblical and ancient events. This was immediately dismissed as foolishness by the scientific establishment. He also upset historians by proposing a recrafting of the chronologies of ancient Egypt based upon celestial time markers. It is interesting to note that his outlandish claims of asteroid and comet impacts, for which Velikovsky was so criticized, are accepted now in the history of the solar system and Earth.

What is important is that Velikovsky elevated the observations of people who lived through those events to the level of scientific consideration, rather than mythological storytelling. While some of his analysis lacked scientific propriety and was not completely correct, he did bring the concept of catastrophism into the mainstream. The fact that some of his ideas are still being discussed is in itself is a testament to his vision.

Mainstream science today agrees that objects, like asteroids and comets, have struck the Earth, and many of the other planets, many times in the past. A comet that hit or merely passed the Earth at close range could cause tidal waves, rocks raining from the sky, and rivers appearing to turn to blood. Upon my first reading of his *Worlds in Collision*, I realized the great value in viewing the people who lived through these events as valid observers. Then I could try to correlate biblical events to actual occurrences. Even if many of Velikovsky's explanations were farfetched, his efforts to apply scientific method to what had been previously dismissed as myth and allegory were more than enough to make me cherish his work. His approach played a great part in how I directed my own research in the years that followed.

Once we raise witnesses in early history to the level of credible observers, it becomes possible to visualize what actually happened by analyzing those observations.

Early humans had questions. Theology and the as-yet-undeveloped tenets of science had answers. According to Exodus, Moses parted the Red Sea. If the account is real, there are two possible explanations: One is a possible scenario based on science. In the chaos of the solar system, comets and asteroids are always in complex motion near planetary trajectories. Perhaps one flew by the Earth just as the Hebrews were ready to cross the sea to escape the pharaoh's legions. It could have created a sudden tidal surge that pulled the sea to one side while they crossed. As they reached the other side, the tidal pull from the receding object fell, and the water surged back into the sea and drowned the Egyptians.

The fact that these objects would have been set into motion far before the actual event is interesting in itself. Did predestination drive the Hebrews, the comet, and the Egyptians to the same point in space and time? Was it part of God's plan?

The second explanation is that God did it by magic. If we dismiss magic as an explanation then God could act upon the world using only natural rather than supernatural means.

In ancient times, the blending of theology and science was natural. As observations were normalized, religion used them to support the hypothetical existence of gods, and then one God. Consider the substantial credibility gained by an Egyptian priest who predicted the flooding of the Nile as shown by the gods as stars in the night sky.

Ancient civilizations tried to make sense of their existence and the surrounding world. Science and theology both meet our need to know and understand everything. The schism between science and religion occurred more for political reasons than because the two worldviews were antithetical. When organized religion felt that science was threatening dogma and canon, such as the worldview of Copernicus and Galileo, it lashed out against new ideas. Since the church had codified a cosmology in which the Earth was the center of the universe, the proposal that it orbited the Sun was more than just an interesting new hypothesis. It was an event capable of shattering the entire church culture.

Science formed the basis of all civilizations and culminated in a God-centered set of religions. Suddenly, they were branded as heretics by trying to continue the same process of hypothesis, experiment, and analysis.

The feud raged for hundreds of years, through the Industrial Revolution, the rise of empires, and the coming of the age of reason. The printing press made knowledge common and allowed ideas to grow and spread. New ideas led to new science and even new religion. One could argue that the Protestant Reformation was a direct result of the Gutenberg printing press turning out tens of thousands of Bibles.

In the twentieth century, something interesting occurred. Science had evolved into a natural philosophy known as physics. A greater understanding of the big and the small quickly led to cosmology and quantum mechanics. At that point, science began to cross back into territory long abandoned to theology.

The circle was complete. Humanity's quest for knowledge and wisdom had taken separate paths for centuries. This pursuit was now converging into a new philosophical framework. Physics is the continuation of the process begun by the first humans who asked, "What is the world?", "How did I get here?", and "What does it all mean?"

Wise men, priests, and scientists throughout history shared in the effort to answer these questions and all the derivative ones. Today, this mission is at the center of the *new* physics as it attempts to answer the greatest of all questions. Physics and theology fulfill the same need in our spirits—the need to know the Creator, the creation, and ourselves.

The impetus of science moving toward a process that requires theological consideration came from two directions. Until the early twentieth century, scientists believed in an eternal and unchanging universe. This model obviated a need for questions about how the universe began. Great thinkers such as Newton and Einstein believed in an eternal universe, but were troubled that this model did not take gravitation into account. Gravity as a purely attractive force would eventually lead to a contraction and eventual collapse of all matter in the universe!

Newton solved this problem by invoking God. As a part of his active role in the creation, he was given janitorial duties that included keeping objects apart. The young Einstein was reluctant to invoke God in his general relativity theory. Yet he still needed to resolve the mechanism by which gravity would not collapse the universe. Einstein invented the idea of an *antigravity* force. When added to his equations, it allowed the universe to be eternal. This was a total *fudge factor* with no basis in evidence, measurement, or intuition. Einstein later referred to this line of thinking as the "greatest blunder of his career." As it turned out, Einstein's fudge factor was actually correct as born out in modern theory.

The second law of thermodynamics posed a second major problem with an eternal universe. Simply put, it states that in a closed system, the total amount of chaos/entropy/disorder will increase with the passage of time. Obviously, this means that the eternal, unchanging universe is impossible. This law provides a clear direction to the so-called "Arrow of Time" in which the universe has a past (with less entropy) and a future (when all order will be reduced to chaos). This implies that the universe has a beginning and an end. If this is true, God is assigned another role, the great clock winder. According to thermodynamics, he created ordered systems at the beginning that run down over time.

In the 1920s, all was well in cosmology, and science did not have to invoke God as part of its fundamental dogma. Then a small group of cosmologists proposed a theory that the universe began in an enormous explosion from a cosmic super egg ten or twenty billion years ago. This theory did not need a magical repulsive force. It led to a dynamic, time-evolving view of the universe, rather than the unchanging state of the eternal model. These ideas eventually led to the big bang theory.

Big science completely rejected this model at first. One of the formulators of the theory, Georges Lemaître, was both a cosmologist and an ordained priest, which gave the establishment a way to dismiss his work. They cited his theology and strong need to bring a creator into the process as his reasons for putting forward the idea. Even Einstein ridiculed "the Priest's physics abominable," which certainly did not help the acceptance of the new concept.

In 1929, Edwin Hubble, an astronomer working at Mount Wilson Observatory in California discovered that all observable galaxies were moving away from each other as if they had been ejected from a common explosion. The universe was deemed to be expanding. "Into what?" you may ask. We will return to this question in a later chapter.

Hubble's work convinced Einstein to embrace the expanding universe model, making the statement: "This is the most beautiful and satisfactory explanation of creation to which I have ever listened." After Einstein publicly admitted his repulsive force was a blunder, the world began to accept the new model.

In a series of experiments designed in 1965, a final discovery convinced the scientific establishment that the big bang theory was correct. Arno Penzias and Robert Wilson, who were employed by Bell Labs, were calibrating a very sensitive horn antenna to detect extremely low levels of microwave radiation. In the process, they discovered a background noise in the system, not unlike the static that we hear on a radio. Fearing that it would mask any low levels of radiation, they began work to remove the noise. They cleaned out bird droppings in the horn, polished the surface, cooled the detector, and tuned the electronics, all to no avail. Finally, they pointed the antenna to space to find out where the noise originated.

Once all other possibilities had been ruled out, only one explanation remained: the noise was coming from space. Not only that but also it was exactly the same no matter where the antenna was pointed. Utilizing well-known physics (blackbody radiation spectra), they realized that the noise would be produced for a radiator at 2.7 degrees on the Kelvin scale (-276.85 Centigrade).

Once this was published, it came to light that a group of theoretical physicists at Princeton had predicted that the big bang would have left a residual microwave background radiation. In fact, the Princeton group was planning an experiment to detect it. The predictions at Princeton matched the measurements at Bell Labs! In a remarkable coincidence, the theory and experiment complemented each other even though they arrived at their results using completely different paths. Penzias and Wilson won the Nobel Prize in physics in 1978 for their accidental discovery.

This process of hypothesis, challenge, experimental verification, and if proven, eventual acceptance of a theory is fundamental to science. The big bang has been accepted by all scientists as the best model to explain the universe as we know it today. The completeness of the theory is supported by the observation of an expanding universe. The predicted calculations were verified by observation of the background radiation as a remnant of the explosion of the big bang. It also was in agreement with other universal laws, such as the second law of thermodynamics.

At this point, the paths of science and religion were inextricably coupled.

A few years ago, astronomers realized that the expansion of the universe was not slowing down, as one would expect if there were only an attractive force of gravity. Instead, the expansion is actually speeding up. Distant galaxies are accelerating away from each other! This requires a huge repulsive force, which theoreticians are now attributing to a new entity, dark matter.

Earlier, we talked about Einstein's fudge factor, which he added to keep the general relativity equations from leading to a collapse of the universe. He called it his greatest blunder. As it turns out, Einstein's "greatest blunder" may not have been so wrong after all!

What follows is a quick guide to cosmology and the creation of the universe, in which I will describe the entire creation from the beginning of time to the end, including the development of life. This is a bold endeavor. If it succeeds, you will know everything there is to know about everything. That should make you a very popular guest at dinner and cocktail parties. Some of you may glaze over at the magnitude of numbers and concepts. In any case, what I want you to take away from this section is its completeness and choreographed beauty. How amazing that we can tell such a story without invoking any magic or falling into any inconstancies or holes!

The very early universe formed in tiny fractions of the first second. At this point, we need to introduce a small amount of mathematical notation; the negative powers of ten. In this method, numbers like .001 are written as 10^{-3}, which means that you need to move the decimal point to the left. With that in mind, let's consider the time line of the universe.

The cosmological time line for the creation is fairly well understood. Scientists believe that the universe was once a point with no actual size. We call this point a singularity. Time begins. The current leading candidate for the theory of everything (string theory) identifies ten dimensions. Six of them collapsed and curled up into immeasurable loops, leaving the four dimensions we know. This defines space.

Time and space were created in 0 to 10^{-43} seconds. This number has forty-two zeros to the right of the decimal point (.000000000000000000000000000000000000000000 0001). The universe is now 10^{-43} seconds old. As it turns out, this is the smallest unit of time that can be measured. This is known as Planck time, defined as the time it would take a photon traveling at the speed of light (3×10^8 meters per second) to cross a distance equal to the Planck length (about 1.616×10^{-35} meters). The four fundamental forces in the universe—gravity, electromagnetic, strong, and weak—are born as a single unified field. This is the moment where gravity, one of these four fundamental forces, separates from the other forces.

As the clock moves to 10^{-36} seconds, the strong nuclear force, which holds the nuclei of atoms together, separates from the remaining three forces. For the next short interval (10^{-36}–10^{-32} seconds) the universe expands rapidly.

In the next period (10^{-32}–10^{-5} seconds), the universe fills with primary particles: quarks, antiquarks, and electrons. Then the quarks and antiquarks combine and annihilate each other! Since the numbers of quarks exceed the number of antiquarks by a ratio of 1,000,000,001 to 1,000,000,000, the symmetry breaks down. If these two numbers had been equal, all the particles would have annihilated each other, and there would be no matter at all. The excess of surviving quarks will make up all the matter that exists in the universe. Questions arise: Why did this *dis*-symmetry arise? Is this proof of the hand of God?

Coming up on 10^{-12} seconds the final two forces separate from each other. Electromagnetism, which controls the attraction of negatively and positively charged particles, becomes separate from the weak nuclear force, which controls radioactive decay.

At the ripe old age 10^{-5} seconds, the universe cools to 1,000,000,000,000 degrees Kelvin. This allows quarks to combine and form protons and neutrons, the building blocks of atomic nuclei.

From one second to three minutes, the universe continues to cool, allowing protons and neutrons to combine to form the nuclei of future atoms.

For the next three thousand years, the electromagnetic energy produced during the annihilation of quarks and antiquarks dominates the forces of gravity.

From three thousand years after the creation to the present, matter becomes the primary source of gravity. Matter begins to clump with the aid of large amounts of exotic or dark matter. This matter interacts weakly with electromagnetic energy, but is able to clump with itself through gravity, even with the domination of electromagnetic energy.

As the universe reaches three hundred thousand years of age, the continued expansion and cooling allow matter and electromagnetic energy to decouple. The nuclei of atoms are able to capture electrons to form complete atoms of hydrogen, helium, and lithium.

At around the two-hundred-million-year mark, galaxy formation begins as matter continues to clump.

Gravity continues to aggregate matter into stars, which are composed of hydrogen, helium, and lithium. These are the only elements in the universe at this time. The force of gravity squeezes the cores of these stars to the point where nuclear fusion occurs, and the force of the exploding core is balanced by the force of gravity.

These first-generation stars light up the universe. For the next several billion years, the stars go through a number of cycles in which gravity squeezes matter in a fusion furnace. As most of the hydrogen/helium/lithium fuel is converted to heavier elements, fusion stops, gravity compresses the core even more, raising temperatures to the point where fusion of higher elements begins. This process continues until the core runs out of the element iron; at which time, no further fusion is possible. The core collapses cataclysmically and a supernova occurs, in which all the rest of the elements of the periodic table are created.

The remnant of this explosion is a cloud containing all the elements. After around nine billion years, our solar system forms from this dirty cloud. The planets form with a new star at its center, our Sun.

As the universe reached its ten billionth birthday, the primordial Earth already had life on it. DNA, the great mystery, eventually leads to speciation and the development of an almost infinite variety of living things—including human beings.

Not only is the universe expanding but also the rate of expansion is increasing. This requires some elegant other stuff, which we call dark matter. Prior to the discovery that the universe was expanding at an ever-increasing rate, the prevailing view was that the expansion was caused by the big bang explosion itself. In that model, it was expected that the force of gravity, which was attractive, would eventually slow the expansion, and eventually reverse it! This is analogous to what happens when you throw a ball up into the air. It leaves your hand at its greatest speed, slows as it rises, and eventually stops at its highest point. The ball then falls back to the ground at an ever-increasing speed. All scientists thought that the end of the universe would be a big crunch. The expansion would slow due to gravity, then the expansion would stop, and finally the universe would fall back into itself. Many believed that when all matter fell back to the center, there would be a huge explosion, possibly leading to a new big bang, and thus a new universe.

Alas, now the future is less exciting. The universe will disperse. Entropy will win. The universe will end eventually. Please do not fret! This will not happen for a trillion years.

As a result of this section, you know that you were actually made from particles produced in the core of the first-generation stars. Other than the hydrogen, helium, and lithium created in the early universe, this is true of everything else in the universe. You are made of stardust… literally!

You also know that this picture is so complete. There are hundreds of books that you could read for more detail, but the essential point is that we know all this. There are no discontinuous gaps or magic or hand-waving stories here.

As long as we start with the moment after the big bang, cosmology provides answers to most of our questions about creation. Note the word "after." This sets an important boundary condition in the entire philosophical foundation of relating cosmology to creation.

Now we arrive at the bigger question: "Why does cosmology lead to theological foundations?"

Cosmology is a profound and interesting discipline. As we have shown in our quick overview, we now have a great deal of confidence about the process of creation from after the big bang to the end of time. We know all about how matter and energy separated and became the stuff to make galaxies, stars, and planets. We know how planets form and evolve. We know how stars age and die. We know that we are made of the stuff of first-generation stars. We understand the mechanisms of life.

We know a great deal.

Yet there is a gaping hole in our knowledge, more like a wall than a hole...

The question seems simple: "What was there *before* the big bang?" At the moment of the big bang time began. Everything that happens *after* the big bang is knowable. Since time was not yet underway, what does *before* mean? Without time how does the state go from *before* to *after*.

We don't know. We can't know. Because our semantics are bound by our ability to perceive and measure, this is the wall at which science ends, and theology begins.

"Where did the universe come from?" is another of the great questions, yet it includes ambiguous references. Space also did not exist until after the big bang, so there was no *place* to come *from*.

Did the universe come from *nothing* or *something* or has it always been?

And then there is the greatest question of all: "What set the creation into motion? How did it get triggered?"

Clearly we have crossed into the area where me must leave science behind and probe theology for answers.

Since time and space did not exist before the moment of creation, the agent of creation must exist outside of space and time! Think about that. There must be a trigger to change the state of *nothing* to *something*. The agent cannot be derivative of that which is created.

Outside of space and time!

As if that were not sufficiently mind-blowing, ponder this:

In the first few trillionths of a second after the big bang, physics and all the laws of nature were formulated. All the constants of the universe were defined. Every rule governing every event that would ever happen anywhere in the universe was created in the first tiniest, almost immeasurable, fragment of the newly created time.

Mathematics, the very language of creation, popped into existence. Everything worked, and continues to work! There is a simple beauty to the forms of equations and an inherent simplicity to the underlying mechanisms.

And, as we have said earlier, we can understand all of it. How can this be?

More importantly, why is all this so?

We are entering a dimension of thought and wisdom. There is a signpost up ahead. We are entering the zone where science finds God. And we begin our deeper look at Genesis.

Cosmology and Theology
Converge in Genesis

Cosmology has given us a powerful, detailed, process and chronology of the history of the universe that is deeply satisfying to the intellect. Yet many philosophical and profound great questions still haunt us: "Where did we come from? Who or what made the world, and how?" All the unanswered, and perhaps unanswerable, questions raised by the mind of the child and the mind of the adult leave us feeling strangely unfulfilled. Our deep need for resolution remains unmet.

The great questions have been part of our minds and cultures throughout our development as a sentient race. All early civilizations met this need by constructing creation myths that ranged from the bizarre to the humorous. By looking at some of these stories, we can gain some perspective as to their creativity and importance in the ancient world. A few stories are included below, and a trip to the Internet and a short Google search will give you access to dozens more.

> In one Egyptian creation myth, the sun god Ra takes the form of Khepri, the scarab god who was usually credited as the great creative force of the universe. Khepri tells us,
>
> "Heaven and earth did not exist. And the things of the earth did not yet exist. I raised them out of Nu, from their stagnant state. I have made things out of that which I have already made, and they came from my mouth."
>
> It seems that Khepri is telling us that in the beginning there is nothing. He made the watery abyss known as Nu, from which he later draws the materials needed for the creation of everything. He goes on to say,
>
> "I found no place to stand. I cast a spell with my own heart to lay a foundation in Maat. I made everything. I was alone. I had not yet breathed the god Shu, and I had not yet spit up the goddess Tefnut. I worked alone."
>
> We learn that by the use of magic Khepri creates land with its foundation in Maat (law, order, and stability). We also learn that from this foundation many things came into being. At this point in time Khepri is alone.
>
> "The sun, which was called the eye of Nu, was hidden by the children of Nu. It was a long time before these two deities, Shu and Tefnut were raised

out of the watery chaos of their father, Nu. They brought with them their fathers eye, the sun. Khepri then wept profusely, and from his tears sprang men and women. The gods then made another eye, which probably represents the moon. After this Khepri created plants and herbs, animals, reptiles and crawling things. In the meantime Shu and Tefnut gave birth to Geb and Nut, who in turn gave birth to Osiris and Isis, Seth, Nephthys."

Ancient Egyptian Creation Myth

"In the beginning there was the void. And the void was called Ginnungagap. What does Ginnungagap mean? Yawning gap, beginning gap, gap with magical potential, mighty gap; these are a few of the educated guesses. Along with the void existed Niflheim the land of fog and ice in the north and Muspelheim the land of fire in the south. There seems to be a bit of confusion as to whether or not these existed after Ginnungagap or alongside of it from the beginning.

"In Niflheim was a spring called Hvergelmir from which the Elivagar (eleven rivers—Svol, Gunnthra, Fiorm, Fimbulthul, Slidr, Hrid, Sylg, Ylg, Vid, Leiptr, and Gioll) flowed. The Elivargar froze layer upon layer until it filled in the northerly portion of the gap. Concurrently the southern portion was being filled by sparks and molten material from Muspelheim.

"The mix of fire and ice caused part of the Elivagar to melt forming the figures Ymir the primeval giant and the cow Audhumla. The cow's milk was Ymir's food. While Ymir slept his under arm sweat begat two frost giants, one male one female, while his two legs begat another male.

"While Ymir was busy procreating Audhumla was busy eating. Her nourishment came from licking the salty ice. Her incessant licking formed the god Buri. He had a son named Bor who was the father of Odin, Vili, and Ve.

"For some reason the sons of Bor decided to kill poor Ymir. His blood caused a flood which killed all of the frost giants except for two, Bergelmir and his wife, who escaped the deluge in their boat.

"Odin, Vili, and Ve put Ymir's corpse into the middle of ginnungagap and created the earth and sky from it. They also created the stars, sun, and moon from sparks coming out of Muspelheim.

"Finally, the brothers happened upon two logs lying on the beach and created the first two humans Ask [Ash] and Embla [vine?] from them."

Norse Myths of the Creation

The great civilization of China developed the following explanation for the Creation:

"In the beginning, the heavens and earth were still one and all was chaos. The universe was like a big black egg, carrying Pan Gu inside itself. After 18 thousand years Pan Gu woke from a long sleep. He felt suffocated, so he took up a broadax and wielded it with all his might to crack open the egg.

The light, clear part of it floated up and formed the heavens, the cold, turbid matter stayed below to form earth. Pan Gu stood in the middle, his head touching the sky, his feet planted on the earth. The heavens and the earth began to grow at a rate of ten feet per day, and Pan Gu grew along with them. After another 18 thousand years, the sky was higher, the earth thicker, and Pan Gu stood between them like a pillar 9 million li in height so that they would never join again.

"When Pan Gu died, his breath became the wind and clouds, his voice the rolling thunder. One eye became the sun and on the moon. His body and limbs turned to five big mountains and his blood formed the roaring water. His veins became far-stretching roads and his muscles fertile land. The innumerable stars in the sky came from his hair and beard, and flowers and trees from his skin and the fine hairs on his body. His marrow turned to jade and pearls. His sweat flowed like the good rain and sweet dew that nurtured all things on earth. According to some versions of the Pan Gu legend, his tears flowed to make rivers and radiance of his eyes turned into thunder and lighting. When he was happy the sun shone, but when he was angry black clouds gathered in the sky. One version of the legend has it that the fleas and lice on his body became the ancestors of mankind."

Ancient Chinese Creation Mythology

And then there is Genesis, which many believe is just another creation myth. Yet it alone follows the story of the creation in cosmology fairly well. Not only is there good alignment between the two visions but also there is also a clear concept of time divisions (days) and of the order in which things happened. Many cite the obvious discrepancy between the lengths of time between the *days*. Clearly, the day discussed in Genesis is not a twenty-four hour Earth day. The Earth, Sun, and moon were not even created until the fourth day. Common modern practice is far more reasonable: to assume that the Genesis day is really an epoch of time, possibly billions of Earth years long.

Dr. Gerald Schroeder in his essay, "The Age of the Universe," offers the following analysis: "There are early Jewish sources that tell us that the calendar in the Bible is in two parts (even predating Leviticus Rabba which goes back almost 1500 years and says it explicitly). In the closing speech that Moses makes to the people, he says if you want to see the fingerprint of God in the universe, "consider the days of old, the years of the many generations" (Deut. 32:7). Nachmanides, in the name of Kabbalah, says, "Why does Moses break the calendar into two parts: 'The days of old, and the years of the many generations?' Because, 'Consider the days of old' is the Six Days of Genesis. 'The years of the many generations' is all the time from Adam forward."

> "Moses says you can see God's fingerprint on the universe in one of two ways. Look at the phenomenon

of the Six Days, and the development of life in the universe that is overwhelming. Or if that doesn't impress you, then just consider society from Adam forward—the phenomenon of human history. Either way, you will find the imprint of God."

Thus the idea that time is split into two different types of time metrics in Genesis is quite obvious and makes sense logically.

The history of everything naturally falls into two distinct frameworks. Remember that no sentient beings existed in the very early moments of creation. In fact, they did not appear until just a few seconds ago on the scale of cosmic time. Thus the writers of Genesis somehow divined the stories about creation and the evolution of the galaxies, stars, and planets.

Once human beings existed, they began to record oral and written histories about events they actually observed. Clearly the New Testament reads like a news report of occurrences around Jesus Christ. It was written by several different reporters, known as Apostles, who were giving first-person accounts of what they saw.

Dr. Schroeder goes on to look at the actual meanings of the original Genesis texts:

> Another example is Genesis 1:5, which says, 'There is evening and morning, Day One.' That is the first time that a day is quantified: evening and morning.

Nachmanides discusses the meaning of evening and morning. Does it mean sunset and sunrise? It would certainly seem to.

But Nachmanides points out a problem with that. The text says, 'There was evening and morning Day One...evening and morning a second day... evening and morning a third day.' Then on the fourth day, the sun is mentioned. Nachmanides says that any intelligent reader can see an obvious problem. How do we have a concept of evening and morning for the first three days if the sun is only mentioned on Day Four? There is a purpose for the sun appearing only on Day Four, so that as time goes by and people understand more about the universe, you can dig deeper into the text.

Nachmanides says the text uses the words 'Vayehi Erev'—but it doesn't mean 'there was evening.' He explains that the Hebrew letters Ayin, Resh, Bet—the root of 'erev'—is chaos. Mixture, disorder. That's why evening is called 'erev,' because when the sun goes down, vision becomes blurry. The literal meaning is 'there was disorder' The Torah's word for 'morning'—'boker'—is the absolute opposite. When the sun rises, the world becomes 'bikoret,' orderly, able to be discerned. That's why the sun needn't be mentioned until Day Four. Because from erev to boker is a flow from disorder to order, from chaos to cosmos. That's something any scientist will testify never happens in an unguided system. Order never arises from disorder spontaneously and remains orderly. Order always degrades to chaos unless the environment recognizes the order and locks it in to preserve it. There must be a guide to the system. That's an unequivocal statement.

The Torah wants us to be amazed by this flow, starting from chaotic plasma and ending up with a symphony of life. Day-by-day the world progresses to higher and higher levels. Order out of disorder. It's pure thermodynamics. And it's stated in terminology of 3000 years ago.

Genesis could have said, "God made the universe by magic, all at once," but it didn't. It could have been poetic and allegorical, with gods and animals working in weird and indecipherable ways to create the universe. Remember the Norse? While Ymir slept his underarm sweat begat two frost giants, one male and one female, while his two legs begat another male." Underarm sweat! Where could science even begin to rationalize such a story?

In complete fairness, I should point out that the way we measure the age of the universe is subject to one piece of cosmic irony. While society still argues about whether or not the Earth (and the universe) is ten thousand years old or billions of years old, there is no actual absolute measure. In fact, if God created the universe ten minutes ago, placing fossils in the rocks and placing galaxies in space with light traveling from them as if it had left them hundreds of millions of years ago, how would we know?

If God set things up so that it appeared old to all of our measuring tools (carbon dating and redshifts), that is what we would measure. Our minds could have included a bunch of memories and a set of knowledge to make us think we have lived a long time! Think about it—there is no physical test that could refute this idea.

I do not believe that the whole universe was created ten minutes ago, or even ten thousand years ago. Creation is far more elegant following the series of evolutionary processes that we discussed earlier. The staged creation, as recited in Genesis and analyzed in cosmology, is something that I find more likely, even though it is no more provable than the instant universe model. Many authors have posed parallel analyses of Genesis and cosmology. Gerald Schroeder's *Genesis and the Big Bang* is worth reading for its detail and completeness.

It would be helpful to look at all thirty-one verses of the original text of Genesis (translated into English in the King James Version) to see how these ideas align.

> In the beginning God created the heaven and the earth.
>
> And the earth was without form, and void; and darkness was upon the face of the deep. And the Spirit of God moved upon the face of the waters.
>
> And God said, Let there be light: and there was light.
>
> And God saw the light, that it was good: and God divided the light from the darkness.

And God called the light Day, and the darkness he called Night. And the evening and the morning were the first day.

And God said, Let there be a firmament in the midst of the waters, and let it divide the waters from the waters.

And God made the firmament, and divided the waters which were under the firmament from the waters which were above the firmament: and it was so.

And God called the firmament Heaven. And the evening and the morning were the second day.

And God said Let the waters under the heaven be gathered together unto one place, and let the dry land appear: and it was so.

And God called the dry land Earth; and the gathering together of the waters called the Seas: and God saw that it was good.

And God said, Let the earth bring forth grass, the herb yielding seed, and the fruit tree yielding fruit after his kind, whose seed is in itself, upon the earth: and it was so.

And the earth brought forth grass, and herb yielding seed after his kind, and the tree yielding fruit, whose seed was in itself, after his kind: and God saw that it was good.

And the evening and the morning were the third day.

And God said, Let there be lights in the firmament of the heaven to divide the day from the night; and let them be for signs, and for seasons, and for days, and years:

And let them be for lights in the firmament of the heaven to give light upon the earth: and it was so.

And God made two great lights; the greater light to rule the day, and the lesser light to rule the night: he made the stars also.

And God set them in the firmament of the heaven to give light upon the earth,

And to rule over the day and over the night, and to divide the light from the darkness: and God saw that it was good.

And the evening and the morning were the fourth day.

And God said, Let the waters bring forth abundantly the moving creature that hath life, and fowl that may fly above the earth in the open firmament of heaven.

And God created great whales, and every living creature that moveth, which the waters brought forth abundantly, after their kind, and every winged fowl after his kind: and God saw that it was good.

And God blessed them, saying, Be fruitful, and multiply, and fill the waters in the seas, and let fowl multiply in the earth.

And the evening and the morning were the fifth day.

And God said, Let the earth bring forth the living creature after his kind, cattle, and creeping thing, and beast of the earth after his kind: and it was so.

And God made the beast of the earth after his kind, and cattle after their kind, and every thing that creepeth upon the earth after his kind: and God saw that it was good.

And God said, Let us make man in our image, after our likeness: and let them have dominion over the fish of the sea, and over the fowl of the air, and over the cattle, and over all the earth, and over every creeping thing that creepeth upon the earth.

So God created man in his own image, in the image of God created he him; male and female created he them.

And God blessed them, and God said unto them, Be fruitful, and multiply, and replenish the earth, and subdue it: and have dominion over the fish of the sea, and over the fowl of the air, and over every living thing that moveth upon the earth.

And God said, Behold, I have given you every herb bearing seed, which is upon the face of all the earth, and every tree, in the which is the fruit of a tree yielding seed; to you it shall be for meat.

And to every beast of the earth, and to every fowl of the air, and to every thing that creepeth upon the earth, wherein there is life, I have given every green herb for meat: and it was so.

And God saw every thing that he had made, and, behold, it was very good. And the evening and the morning were the sixth day.

Let's examine the verses more closely to see if they align with modern views.

In Genesis 1:1–5, the concepts of a beginning, an action of creating and the well-known "Let there be light!" agree well with our picture of a big bang. This is in fact the great synthesis of the two visions, which finally brought even reluctant scientists to the conclusion that the existence of a beginning allowed (or required) the existence of a creator.

Genesis 1:6–8 discusses the separation of *heaven* (firmament) from the *waters*. In cosmology, the universe developed by separation and cooling, leading to the formation of matter and gas clouds and then galaxies.

When we get to Genesis 1:9–13, we have the formation of the planets (Earth) and the seas. A discussion of the creation of nonanimal life (including the idea of reproduction by seeds) follows. We believe that prebiotic life led to microorganisms long before there were animals. Not a perfect match, but still within correct sequence.

On the fourth day (Genesis 1:14–19), God arranges for the lights of the Sun and moon to shine down to Earth and to fix periods of day and seasons. During the development of the planet, there were often thick clouds obscuring the sky. At this point, there is an atmosphere, day and nights, seasons, and water. The stage is set for an explosion of the greatest miracle—life.

The next great stage (Genesis 1:19–23) is the creation and proliferation of life in the sea. While Genesis also talks about birds, what I find most interesting is that life fills the sea before it goes onto the land. The fifth day ends with the seas teeming with life. The vision also indicates that the skies are teeming with flying life. Consider the fact that birds are now thought to be related to dinosaurs. Since the ecosystem could not yet support birds on the land, perhaps these might have been flying reptile fish!

The sixth day was especially good. God creates all the animals. "Let the earth bring forth the living creature after his kind, cattle, and creeping thing, and beast of the earth after his kind." The text also makes a very strong point that this life is *after his kind*, which is clearly a reference to the concept of species. For those who reject Darwin on biblical grounds, consider that Genesis describes life as arising in order (simple, complex, sea, and land) and by speciation. Life culminates in the creation of Adam and Eve, who are given dominion over all the other creatures and plants. Human beings are the highest creation. "God created man in his own image, in the image of God created he him; male and female created he them." God made man and woman the caretakers of the world and commanded them to be fruitful and multiply.

Clearly the arrival of humanity in the history of the world was a huge event. As tool users and thinking beings, humans have indeed been fruitful and multiplied across the planet. In Genesis, the first man was created in a pure state. The tale then continues with the story of Adam and Eve in the Garden of Eden.

Once man was comfortable in the garden, God stated the following restrictions: "And the LORD God commanded the man, saying, of every tree of the garden thou mayest freely eat: But of the tree of the knowledge of good and evil, thou shalt not eat of it: for in the day that thou eatest thereof thou shalt surely die."

What does this story say about man, created in God's image, and about his role for all of time? Why was he forbidden from eating the fruit of the tree of knowledge? Why are we led to believe that knowledge leads to evil and death?

As a scientist, I have dedicated my life to the pursuit of knowledge. Is knowledge evil? Is science? With more careful thought, we realize that knowledge—without morality and ethics—is dangerous. Perhaps the first human beings were not yet ready to have the power that knowledge brings. Indeed the human race still may not be ready.

Science faces this challenge continuously. Should we do things just because we can? Before we understand all the implications? Thus far, our knowledge has brought war, death, the destruction of the environment, and the extinction of entire species. Today, scientists are on the edge of almost godlike powers in fields such as biology, genetics, extending life, and cloning. At the end of the spectrum, we can build nuclear weapons that would kill billions and design plagues that could rival any horrors.

Perhaps, this divinely inspired allegory is the great message of our history! This may be a critical juncture in our civilization. Our hope is that someday all of us will have developed a level of morality and ethics needed to use for the good of all the incredible power gained by our abilities and knowledge.

If not...The future might not be all that we hope that it can be.

Theology and science both fill a human need to understand life, the universe, and everything. The creation myth in Genesis is too close to our scientific understanding to be coincidental. Through the model of the big bang and the expanding universe, science has returned to theology. Does it suffice to understand everything after the big bang? To believe in a creator that must have specific properties to account for what we know?

It certainly is enough for me.

Catastrophism and Chronology: How Old is Civilization?

The Earth is very old.

Seemingly a simple statement, yet controversy about this point has raged for ages in the war between science and theology. Some argue that Genesis should be read literally. Creation lasted seven days, and then chronology should be constructed by counting the generations and histories in the Old Testament. Jewish tradition considers this as the 5769th year since the creation of the universe. According to the Eastern Orthodox Church calendar, the world was created on September 1, 5509, BC.

In the Roman Catholic Church, Archbishop James Usher (1581–1656) proposed the date of creation as Sunday, October 23, 4004, BC in the Julian calendar. He carefully placed the first day of creation, and hence the exact time of creation, at the previous nightfall! This tells you something about the theological importance of creation.

According to Hindu scripture, the universe undergoes endless cycles of creation. Existence is divided into four *yugas* (ages) totaling exactly 4,320,000 years, to be followed by dissolution. They believe the current universe was created about 3,893,100 years ago and is expected to dissolve about 426,900 years from now.

The Mayan calendar dates the creation of the Earth to August 11, or August 13, 3114, BC (establishing that date as the zeroth day of the Long Count 13.0.0.0.0).

Modern scientists consider the universe to be about fourteen plus billion, and the Earth about 4.5 billion years old. In view of many opinions about the age of everything, what is interesting is that almost all cultures agree that there was a beginning and that it was a long time ago.

As we discussed, earlier history has two epochs: one is prehumanity and therefore devoid of experience-based information and the second is the history of the world since sentient beings were able to observe and record experiences using oral or written tradition.

Scriptural traditions lead us to believe that the second epoch is on the order of five to ten thousand years. In addition, many other global mythologies have detailed important events.

A number of striking similarities in stories of early civilizations defy dismissal as pure myth. Ancient peoples were intelligent. Early civilizations established cities, agricultures, arts, and governments. They used written and oral communication, supported trade and commerce, and developed education. Why are we so ready to minimize recorded observations as myths, parables, or allegories?

In the twenty-first century, we find ourselves a violent universe and solar system. We can look at our own moon through binoculars or telephoto lens and see the effect of cosmic bombardment. Larger telescopes can observe impact craters across Mars, Venus, Mercury, and the moons of Jupiter and Saturn.

Scientific observation has shown that objects from space have struck the Earth many times in our past. Dinosaurs were probably wiped out by an asteroid impact about sixty-five million years ago. Earth might look like the moon except that water and weather have eroded and smoothed surface features. Active geological forces, such as plate tectonics and volcanism, also mask all but the largest craters and scars.

National Aeronautics and Space Administration (NASA) and other agencies across the world track asteroids and comets in an attempt to monitor any possible collisions. Have you ever wondered what we would do if they saw one coming!?

Several years ago, two very successful Hollywood films *Armageddon* and *Deep Impact*, shocked viewers with the severity of the problem, but also presented laughably unscientific solutions to saving the world. If an asteroid several miles wide actually did strike the Earth at thousands of miles per hour, it would likely send us the way of the dinosaurs. Sending nuclear missiles or Bruce Willis to destroy objects zooming toward the Earth would be impotent to save us.

Although the numbers of interplanetary objects like asteroids and comets have dropped since the days of the early solar system, cosmic collisions still occur. As recently as 1994, we watched in awe as a huge comet broke into twenty-one pieces and struck Jupiter. The energy release was on the order of tens of millions of nuclear bombs. Had this comet struck the Earth instead, I would not be writing this book and you would no longer be here either.

We are actually greatly indebted to Jupiter. Due to its massive size, the planet's gravitational field pulls many objects into its grasp, thus sweeping up the solar system's rogue objects and keeping our Earth from harm.

Comet Shoemaker-Levy Collision with Jupiter

From July 16 through July 22, 1994, pieces of an object designated as Comet P/Shoemaker-Levy 9 collided with Jupiter. This is the first collision of two solar system bodies ever to be observed, and the effects of the comet impacts on Jupiter's atmosphere have been simply spectacular and beyond expectations. Comet Shoemaker-Levy 9 consisted of at least twenty-one discernible fragments with diameters estimated at up to two kilometers.

Logic tells us that the Earth has been subjected to many impacts since the dinosaur killer sixty-five million years ago. It's possible that some events occurred while ancient civilizations were developing on the Earth. The biblical story of the great flood in Genesis might record an actual cosmic event.

The recent tsunami in South Asia, caused by a strong earthquake on the floor of the Indian Ocean, killed almost a quarter of a million people in just a few hours. In spite of our satellites, cell phones and Internet, millions of people were surprised by a natural event that washed away entire cities without warning.

If a comet or asteroid of significant size hit the Atlantic Ocean off the coast of North Africa about five thousand years ago, around 3100 BC, it would have created a tsunami wave several kilometers high. Imagine the impact as the wave spread out across the Mediterranean, crossing Italy and Greece and slamming into what is now Egypt and Israel. On the other side of the ocean as the waves struck Central and South America. The object may have calved (broke into pieces, like Comet Shoemaker-Levy), carts parts of it to impact elsewhere. These massive tsunami waves would have led to global flooding.

What would the people that time have experienced?

Clearly, such a scenario could explain the descriptions of the deluge in the Bible. A worldwide flood would have affected peoples around the globe. Stories would have been passed down orally from generation to generation, attaining mythological status over time, which is validated by stories told in many cultures very similar to the Genesis Flood. In fact, early historians in Europe, Africa, Asia, Australia, and the Americas recorded hundreds of tales. China's "Hihking

Classic" and Babylon's "Epic of Gilgamesh" are two of the most well known.

Many consider the story told on Tablet XI of the Gilgamesh stones so remarkably like the Genesis's Noah story that it could be either a source or a derivative of that event. It tells of a man commanded by God to build an ark with specific engineering notes. He was to fill it with all sorts of animal and plant life in pairs, ride out a cataclysmic deluge, and then land on a mountain when the waters subsided. The story recorded on the tablet is quite familiar to readers of the Old Testament.

China's "Hihking Classic" includes the passage:

> Fuhi, the reputed founder of Chinese civilization, escaped the waters of a deluge, and reappeared as the first man at the reproduction of a renovated world, accompanied by his wife, his three sons and three daughters.

In the Americas the Aztecs tell the following tale:

> *When the Sun Age came, there had passed 400 years. Then came 200 years, then 76. Then all mankind was lost and drowned and turned to fishes. The water and the sky drew near each other. In a single day all was lost, and Four Flower consumed all that there was of our flesh. The very mountains were swallowed up in the flood,*

and the waters remained, lying tranquil during fifty and two springs. But before the flood began, Titlachahuan had warned the man Nota and his wife Nena, saying, 'Make no more pulque, but hollow a great cypress, into which you shall enter the month Tozoztli. The waters shall near the sky' They entered, and when Titlachahuan had shut them in he said to the man, 'Thou shalt eat but a single ear of maize, and thy wife but one also'. And when they had each eaten one ear of maize, they prepared to go forth, for the water was tranquil (Ancient Aztec document *Codex Chimalpopoca*, translated by Abbe Brasseur de Bourbourg. *The Deluge Story in Stone*, Byron C Nelson, 1931).

Hindu scriptures (the Puranas, and Shatapatha Brahmana, I, 8, 1–6) record:

An avatar of Vishnu in the form of a fish, Matsya, warned Manu of a terrible flood that was to come and that it would wash away all living things. Manu cared for the fish and eventually released it in the sea. There the fish cautioned Manu to build a boat. He did so, and when the flood arrived, the fish towed the ship to safety by a cable attached to his horn. (Alan Dundes [editor], *The Flood Myth*, University of California Press, Berkeley, 1988).

Greek traditions tell of the Flood this way:

> *Zeus sent a flood to destroy the men of the Bronze Age. Prometheus advised his son Deucalion to build a chest. All other men perished except for a few who escaped to high mountains. The mountains in Thessaly were parted, and all the world beyond the Isthmus and Peloponnese was overwhelmed. Deucalion and his wife Pyrrha (daughter of Epimetheus and Pandora), after floating in the chest for nine days and nights, landed on Parnassus. When the rains ceased, he sacrificed to Zeus, the God of Escape. At the bidding of Zeus, he threw stones over his head; they became men, and the stones which Pyrrha threw became women. That is why people are called laoi, from laas, "a stone"* (**Apollodorus: The Library, Sir James G. Frazer (transl.), Harvard University Press, Cambridge, 1921, 1976.**).

An older version of the story told by Hellanicus has Deucalion's ark landing on Mount Othrys in Thessaly. Another account has him landing on a peak, probably Phouka, in Argolis, later called Nemea.

> The Megarians told that Megarus, son of Zeus, escaped Deucalion's flood by swimming to the top of Mount Gerania, guided by the cries of Cranes. An earlier flood was reported to have occurred in the time of Ogyges, founder and king of Thebes.

The flood covered the whole world and was so devastating that the country remained without kings until the reign of Cecrops (Gaster, Theodor H. *Myth, Legend, and Custom in the Old Testament*, Harper and Row, New York, 1969).

The *Timaeus* of Plato refers to the great deluge of all and the *Critias* refers to the great destruction of Deucelion. In addition, the texts report:

Many great deluges have taken place during the nine thousand years since Athens and Atlantis were preeminent. Destruction by fire and other catastrophes was also common. In these floods, water rose from below, destroying city dwellers but not mountain people. The floods, especially the third great flood before Deucalion, washed away most of Athens' fertile soil (Plato, *Timaeus 22*, *Critias* 111–112).

Plato's stories about Atlantis beg another question as well: "Why is recorded history so short? It seems that human beings have had the skills to build civilization for far longer than the five thousand years we know about. Might there have been vast extended cultures as long as ten thousand years ago? Perhaps the Atlantis myth tells of a high civilization destroyed by a natural calamity or war.

To support this idea, we have ancient maps with an unreasonable amount of detail:

Further research by Professor Hapgood, Maps of the Ancient Sea Kings, revealed a treasury of ancient maps in the Library of Congress, many of which show an amazing knowledge of the Earth's true geography at a time when most people did not know that the world was round and when cartographers were apt to fill in blank spaces on maps with drawings of winged cherubs, monsters, or with the annotation 'here be Dragons' The Bauche map (1754) shows the Antarctic continent without ice, divided into two great islands, a fact not reestablished until 1958.... The King Jaime world map shows the Sahara, not as a desert, but as a fertile land of rivers, woods, and lakes, which it once was—before the beginnings of chronicled history (*Atlantis: The Eighth Continent* by Charles Berlitz).

Cataclysmic events seem to be part of nature. Cosmic impacts have all but wiped life off the face of the Earth several times in prehistory. Global tsunamis have deposited fossil marine life high in sedimentary layers on inland mountains. Why not concede that an asteroid could have wiped Atlantis out of existence? Perhaps that led to a worldwide tsunami that may have become the basis of all the flood myths.

Many other events recorded in the Bible and other ancient writings may have actually occurred. At that time theology was science. Ancient civilizations likely explained them as God's direct actions in response to their disobedience. It rained because God made it rain. If fire fell from the sky to smite the enemies of the Hebrews, then God sent it. From a modern viewpoint, could Sodom have been destroyed by a large meteor?

As previously mentioned, Immanuel Velikovsky created a lot of controversy by seeking to expand on this very idea in his book *Worlds in Collision*. What if the events in the Bible, the flood, the parting of the Red Sea, the Sun stopping in the sky as Joshua fought the Battle of Jericho, actually happened?

In the fifty years since Velikovsky, many mainstream historians and archeologists are rethinking chronologies by looking at parallel myths and trying to rationalize a better historical time line. The pyramids in Egypt, Stonehenge, and the temples in Mexico present a clear picture of primitive human beings building complex projects to meet certain goals. With remarkable accuracy, such structures enabled people to track astronomical events. Solstices helped them predict weather and seasons. They were able to foresee meteoric storms and cycles of returning comets.

We know that construction of the pyramids required very advanced building techniques. How were ancient civilizations able to attain such a high level of knowledge? Eric Von Däniken wrote a series of popular books, including *Chariots of the Gods?* attributing the skill in science and engineering shown by the ancient Egyptians and Aztecs to the visit of alien astronauts to Earth! As far out as it sounds, the sophistication of these ancient peoples has always been a mystery.

I think it is more likely that the engineering and construction skills were derived from an undiscovered ancient civilization, perhaps Atlantis itself. The fact that it was all but destroyed thousands of years earlier does not rule out their having passed along knowledge and technology by oral or written traditions. The various theories about the mysteries of ancient people absolutely point to mysteries. Our picture of the past is incomplete.

If a biowarfare bug were unleashed tomorrow morning that would wipe out 99.999% of humankind in a few days, what would people know about us in five or ten thousand years? Our great cities and structures would have long crumbled into dust. All the magnetic and optical media would have slowly aged into chaos. Would our literature, science, and art be all faded and lost? Would enough of our greatness survive as a witness?

Those who lived through such an event would spend generations just struggling to survive, and then they would begin to rebuild. They would rediscover and redevelop most of what they had lost. They might find objects and records that might give them glimpses of what we once were. They would bring back farming, metallurgy, writing, and art.

They would discover electricity and science. They would eventually climb all the way back to where we are today.

But what would be left of the memories of their past?

Mythology.

They would tell stories over the millennia of the great ones, the giants who once ruled the Earth, flew like birds in huge silver-winged craft, and could speak to other great ones on the far side of the world using magical handheld boxes. In religious texts, they might come to believe that these great ones angered God in a way that incurred his wrath and the ultimate punishment. Perhaps God had sent a plague to cleanse the Earth, and that he chose only a few pure humans to survive and rebuild the world to be a better place.

Farfetched? If older and higher civilizations were wiped out by natural disasters or catastrophes that humans caused, why would this scenario not already have occurred? Whether it was Atlantis or some other as of yet undiscovered society, this is exactly what could have happened.

It is my hope that in the next few hundred years, two things will occur: One, of course, is that we as a society survive any manmade disasters or another cosmic impact. The second is that we advance enough in our archeological technology to discover whether or not there were any previous high civilizations that predate our current ancient history. This knowledge would allow us to validate the observations of our perhaps not-so-primitive ancestors handed down to us in the Old Testament and tablets and art of the ancient world. It would be glorious to find a backup site of the great library in Alexandria, which was destroyed in 46 BC. It contained the entire collection of all original copies and a mass of scrolls representing the totality of recorded knowledge of the word at that time. This most catastrophic fire may have destroyed the history of scholarship. Think of the things that we might know today about those early civilizations.

The writings that have survived leave us with a framework of fragments. The Old Testament, the Dead Sea Scrolls, and a handful of partial texts are all that we have left of prehistory. This elevates the historical portions of the Bible as even more valuable insights into their times. They not only speak to issues of faith but also serve as one of the few remaining accounts of ancient events recorded by actual witnesses.

We can apply our modern scientific knowledge and technology in our efforts to understand some of the mysteries our biblical forefathers delegated to faith. However, that in no way diminishes the fact that, as far as we have come, we still need to invoke God as the Creator to complete our worldview. Writers who look to supernatural causes for observed events might recall the words of Arthur C. Clarke, the author of *2001: A Space Odyssey*: "Any sufficiently advanced technology is indistinguishable from magic."

From an Apple to the Moon and Beyond...

Nature and Nature's laws lay hid in night: God said,
Let Newton be! and all was light.

—Alexander Pope

One of the most powerful features of our race is our ability to use our minds to observe, analyze, and derive universal truths. As we examine this process, we will see how simple observations and assumptions can lead not only to the discovery of laws of the universe but also to performing great wonders as well.

The English scholar Sir Isaac Newton was one of the most prominent change agents in human history. He is widely considered one of the most brilliant and influential minds in the development of science and mathematics ever.

His life story is very interesting. His early academic work at Cambridge was far from stellar. "Despite some evidence that his progress had not been particularly good, Newton was elected a scholar on April 28, 1664 and received his bachelor's degree in April 1665. It would appear that his scientific genius had still not emerged, but it did so suddenly when the plague closed the University in the summer of 1665 and he had to return to Lincolnshire. There, in a period of less than two years, while Newton was still under 25 years old, he began revolutionary advances in mathematics, optics, physics, and astronomy."

This is a powerful point in itself. When the university reopened in 1667, let us imagine the young Mr. Newton showing up and announcing, "While I was on vacation, I discovered the calculus, formulated a theory of universal gravitation, defined a series of laws of motion, and developed the science of optics!" Not bad from an underachiever. What did you ever accomplish on spring or summer break?

While Newton's genius erupted during the plague break, science would spend the next several decades absorbing the impact of this one young mind. The calculus opened new methods to study the physical world. By passing sunlight through a prism, he realized that white light was actually made up of all colors. His analytical approach to gravitation provided incredible insight into celestial mechanics.

One mind.

Two years.

Miraculous!

Newton was the first science superstar. Yet his humility survived. Even with all the accolades of Western science falling to him, he is remembered by this quote:

"If I have been able to see further, it was only because I stood on the shoulders of giants" (Sir Isaac Newton).

A triumph of observation and logic, Newton's three laws of motion are fundamental in our understanding of the way things work. In them lies the framework of all dynamics and engineering.

> Acceleration and force are vectors (as indicated by their symbols being displayed in slant bold font); in this law the direction of the force vector is the same as the direction of the acceleration vector.
>
> For every action there is an equal and opposite reaction.
>
> The mythology surrounding Isaac Newton and the apple tree is well known. Newton is pictured as sitting under an apple tree when he noticed an apple fall to the ground.

Pondering the nature of the process, he realized there was a force pulling the apple to Earth. Newton also was aware that the moon was in a circular orbit around the Earth, and thus a force must be in place to pull it from its tendency to move in a straight line, as described by the first law. Extending this concept brought him to the conclusion that the same force that pulled the apple to ground pulled the moon in its orbit.

Thus began the reasoning that led to one of the great pinnacles of early science, the law of gravitation. To say that the laws of the universe are beautiful, elegant, and simple, we need to look only at a few great triumphs of logic and reasoning that led to our understanding of the fundamentals of creation. To the casual observer, the universe appears enormously complex. As it turns, all the processes in the universe can be described by the existence of only four forces. They are gravitation, electromagnetism, the strong, and the weak forces.

In our experiential every day lives, we are aware of the first two. Gravity holds us to the Earth, causes apples to fall from trees, and rules the rotation of the planets around stars and stars around galaxies. It is the prime force in the birth, life, and death of both stars and galaxies.

Open up the mind of the child burning inside you and join me on a thought journey from the apple to the moon.

Think back to a day when you find yourself on a shore of a small lake looking for a fun thing to do. Most of you might pick up a stone and toss it into the lake. You might even try to see how far you could toss the stone, and maybe even reach the other shore.

The child mind would experiment. At first you might toss the stone horizontally (All of these illustrations are mine. My teachers told me I would never be an artist. I intend to send them a copy of this book).

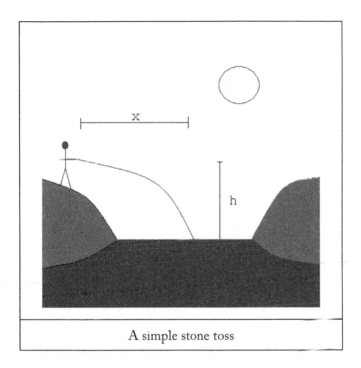

A simple stone toss

The stone moves across a horizontal distance and, at the same time, falls a height of "h" before it hits the water. Even if you throw it really hard, it seems to have a maximum range. You are fighting the gravity for range. The Earth pulls down on the stone at a constant force, which causes it to fall "h" no matter how hard you throw.

If you try throwing it up at various angles, your experiment might look something like this:

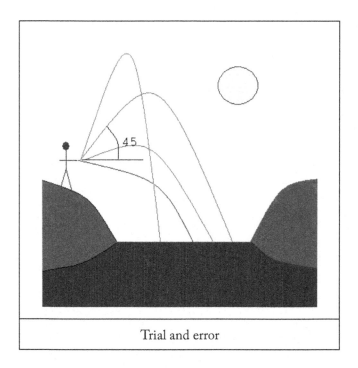

Trial and error

After a few tries, you would discover that the greatest range occurs when you throw the stone at an angle of forty-five degrees. At this angle, part of your throw is used to send the stone up to a greater height. The time of flight is then determined by the time that it takes the stone to fall to earth from the height achieved. At forty-five degrees, you give the stone the greatest possible up velocity as well as the greatest horizontal velocity.

This describes the optimum range, known as a parabolic arc. This principle is common to all trajectories, from golf balls to cannonballs. Mathematics describes this process beautifully, but I have promised to spare you from my scribbles. Yet this principle is one of the way things work in the world.

Let's say that you became obsessed with landing the rock on the far shore. You realize that maximum range is determined by both the angle (forty-five degrees) and the velocity that you throw the stone. As hard as you try, your muscles are only capable of so much. (George Washington is said to have tossed a dollar across the Potomac—I don't buy it!) You run home to make a slingshot. You still do not have enough force to make the crossing. So you run down to the local artillery store and buy cannon.

Not enough power!

You fire the cannon and still fall short! You call the cannon store guy and tell him your problem, and he sells you more powerful gunpowder, capable of giving you a really high-muzzle velocity. You fire the cannon again.

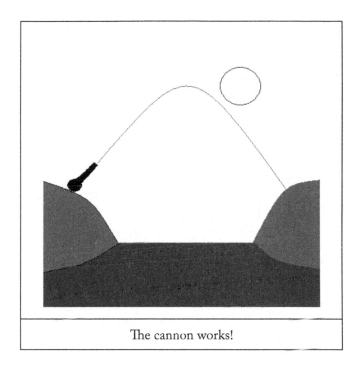

The cannon works!

You succeed! Isn't physics great? You have defined a physical law, discovered the relations of angles and velocity to range, and are ready to enjoy a great career in the mobile infantry.

But you are *really* obsessed. You ask yourself, "What is the greatest possible range on Earth?"

You get the biggest cannon on Earth and load it with the most powerful gunpowder made.

I need to change the scale of my drawing to include the curvature of the Earth.

A cannon on the Earth

Your *law* still holds and the more powerful gunpowder leads to ever-increasing range. But, alas, you reach the end of the cannon's potential at about twenty miles.

Being a bright child, you realize that the velocity could be increased by using an internally propelled cannonball. You use Newton's third law: For every action, there is an equal and opposite reaction. You build an action-reaction projectile, and you call it a rocket-propelled cannonball or RPCB. You are such a clever child.

Your RPCBs give you a greater and greater range.

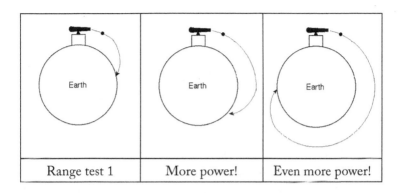

| Range test 1 | More power! | Even more power! |

And then you make an interesting observation. The longer the range, the more curvature of the Earth comes into play.

Then, one day, you bring out your biggest RPCB yet, and an amazing thing occurs.

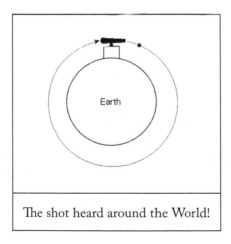

The shot heard around the World!

Your RPCB's range is so far and the Earth's curvature is such that the RPCB falls over the edge. In fact it will never hit the Earth!

You have forced the RPCB into orbit. There is a velocity at which the range of the object bears it over the curvature of the Earth. Even though it is in a constant free fall, it will never hit land!

Amazing! The mathematics of the apple, the stone, the cannonball, and the rocket-propelled cannonball are all the same! The orbits are natural extensions of observations and laws of motion on Earth. Newton realized that the same force pulled the apple to the ground and kept the moon in orbit around the Earth. The moon's velocity moves it around the curvature of the Earth. Thus the moon is falling toward the Earth but never hits it since it falls over the edge. If the moon were to stop or slow down, it would crash into the Earth, which would be very bad.

In the same way, Newton realized, the Earth orbited the Sun, as did all the planets. This celestial ballet is so perfectly choreographed that everything works together, can be described by a single set of mathematics and can be understood. This type of discovery is everywhere in science, a key to understanding the nature of creation.

The science shown in this thought journey took astronauts all the way to the moon in the 1960s during the Apollo program.

Now that you understand orbits, you probably would be able to predict what would happen to your orbiting object if it went even faster. The orbit would get higher but the pull of gravity would still result in free fall and would still be a closed loop.

To get to the moon, we merely needed to increase the orbit to make its highest point to be behind the moon.

First we orbited the capsule.

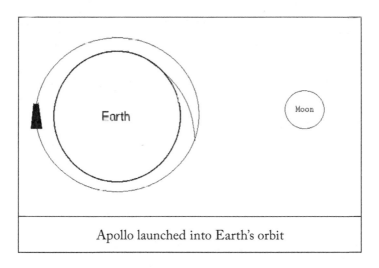

Apollo launched into Earth's orbit

Then we fired additional rockets to raise the orbit to encompass the moon.

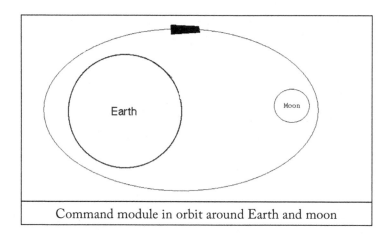

Command module in orbit around Earth and moon

When we reached the far side of the moon, we fired retrorockets to slow us down and drop the orbit to circle only the moon.

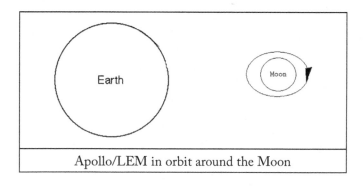

Apollo/LEM in orbit around the Moon

Then we sent the lander down to the moon, leaving the command mobile in lunar orbit.

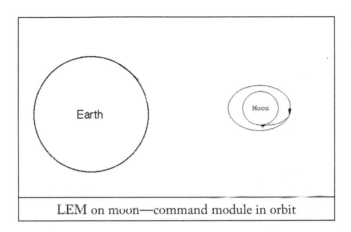

LEM on moon—command module in orbit

Then we launched the ascent stage of the lander to go back into orbit, dock with the command module, which then fired up its engines to raise the orbit back to encircle the Earth.

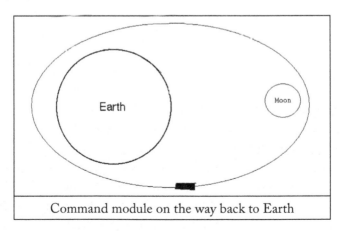

Command module on the way back to Earth

When the Apollo swung back around the Earth, the command module fired its retrorockets for the final time and the small reentry capsule fell back to Earth, landing with the help of parachutes gently in the ocean.

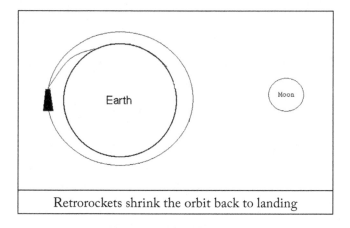

Retrorockets shrink the orbit back to landing

The lunar mission was actually designed using these staged orbits to enable this recovery strategy. A failure in lunar orbit would have been fatal. Once again, all the mathematics involved in these maneuvers are exactly the same as the description of Newton's falling apple. Now you, dear reader, are as smart as a rocket scientist!

On a short note, Apollo 13 had a major system failure on its way to the moon, but as you have seen in the diagrams above, it was actually still in Earth's orbit. While there were many very serious problems on that flight (which were solved quite brilliantly), returning to Earth was not one of them. The orbit that they were in would have returned them to Earth anyway. All they needed were the final retrorockets to lower the command capsule's speed to suborbital velocity and land normally. Luckily the damage to the command module did not damage the capsule's retros.

One final point: the Apollo modules never actually escaped the Earth's gravity. There is a speed at which you could launch a rocket that is so fast that its trajectory will pull it away from the Earth in such a way so that it will never fall back. This is called the escape velocity and is about twenty-five thousand miles per hour. Whenever we launch rockets on missions outside Earth's neighborhood, greater velocities are required. I should note that even on interplanetary trips to Mars, Jupiter, etc., we still use this orbital-size ballet to move through the solar system.

Now you realize that mathematics flow from the "apple to the moon and beyond...."

Time from the Inside and Outside, Flatland, Reality

We live in a universe limited by our physical nature to experience it, but unlimited in our ability to imagine the totality of its wonder.

Our skills of observation and measurement enable us to hypothesize and build theories, which sometimes lead us back to measurement and observation for validation or refutation. Concepts and principles beyond our experiential range do not stymie our quest for understanding. Has anyone ever *seen* an atom or been *near* a black hole to measure its effect on space-time? Has that stopped us from formulating chemistry and nuclear science? Of course not! By measurements and observations, we have expanded our knowledge to reach from the very small, the quantum realm, to the very large, cosmology, and from the beginning to the end of time itself. Quite a stretch for such young and humble creatures to accomplish in just a few thousand years!

Let's try to follow the path that led us to these accomplishments and beyond. Perception is the link between our minds and the world. It enables us to experience things around us and live in the world, especially to measure our surroundings. When we discuss quantum mechanics, we will realize more about the role of measurement in science, but first let's focus on the fundamental way it allows us to organize how we perceive our personal reality.

Dimensions are important as the underlying framework of reality. But what are dimensions and why do they matter? The quick, smart answer you might get from a scientist is that dimensions are "metrics."

The Microsoft Encarta defines:

> METRICS: measurement of the size of something: a measurement of something in one or more directions, for example, its length, width, or height

> SIZE: the size or extent of something (usually used in plural)

> ASPECT: a feature or distinctive part of something

> LIFELIKE QUALITY: a fullness that gives a convincingly lifelike quality

> LEVEL OF REALITY: a level of consciousness, existence, or reality

MATHEMATICS coordinate for space and time: a coordinate used with others to locate a point in space and time

PHYSICS property defining physical quantity: any of a group of properties or magnitudes, such as mass or time that collectively define a physical quantity

Like I said; a metric!

Consider the richness of the concept of dimensions, which allow us to identify size, property, location, and quantity. Dimensions are our connection to the physical universe. Dimensions are the framework and scaffolding of our perceptions. We sense reality within the limitations of the dimensions that we can perceive. That allows us to order and communicate essential information, even beyond the limits of our physical reach.

What does beyond the limits of our physical reach mean?

We humans have built tools to see the complexity of the microscopic world and the birth of galaxies billions of light-years from us. We have derived algebras that involve dimensions that we cannot see or even comprehend. We have used mathematics to codify experience into something loftier, wisdom. The word "geometry" comes from *geo* (Greek for Earth), and *meter* (Greek measure). Imagine the awe early mathematicians must have felt when they discovered the Pythagorean theorem! Here was a way in which one could predict the length of the hypotenuse of a right triangle merely by knowing the length of each of its two legs. Predict, not measure!

The transition of mathematics from measurement to prediction set the stage for the subsequent evolution of science, which allowed the development of science as we know it today. Without the concept of dimensions and measurement, no amount of theory would have led to such powerful results. This may not excite everyone, but it thrills the heart of a scientist!

We live in a universe described by the three physical dimensions we know and love: length, height, and width. The location of a point in space is determined by three numbers (x, y, and z).

But what if the universe is more complex than we can perceive? What if there are six or even ten dimensions? The current string theory suggests just that, as we will consider later.

You may ask, "How can you even understand dimensions that you cannot perceive?"

Answering this requires some mind-stretching exercises. Edwin Abbott, an English clergyman, wrote *Flatland: A Romance of Many Dimensions* under the pseudonym A Square in 1884. Even today, Abbott's delightful book is one of the most utilized sources for visualizing dimensionality. (It is available online and is worth the read.) The story is about a two-dimensional universe in which one of its inhabitants (A Square) discovers the existence of a third dimension. This leads to considerable upheaval in how he perceives of the universe, which and eventually gets him in trouble with the powers that be.

The inhabitants of Flatland are geometric figures (with the exception of women, who are lines). The more sides a figure has, the higher up they are in society. With only one dimension, women can make themselves invisible merely by approaching an observer head on. It is in this geometric hierarchy that Abbott uses *Flatland* to poke fun at Victorian England. Here is the preface from *Flatland*:

> ToThe Inhabitants of SPACE IN GENERALAnd H. C. IN PARTICULARThis Work is DedicatedBy a Humble Native of FlatlandIn the Hope thatEven as he was Initiated into the MysteriesOf THREE dimensionsHaving been previously conversantWith ONLY TWOSo the Citizens of that Celestial RegionMay aspire yet higher and higherTo the Secrets of FOUR FIVE OR EVEN SIX dimensionsThereby contributingTo the Enlargement of THE IMAGINATIONAnd the possible DevelopmentOf that most rare and excellent Gift of MODESTYAmong the Superior RacesOf SOLID HUMANITY

The opening paragraphs continue:

> I CALL our world Flatland, not because we call it so, but to make its nature clearer to you, my happy readers, who are privileged to live in Space.

Imagine a vast sheet of paper on which straight lines, triangles, squares, pentagons, hexagons, and other figures, instead of remaining fixed in their places, move freely about, on or in the surface, but without the power of rising above or sinking below it, very much like shadows—only hard with luminous edges—and you will then have a pretty correct notion of my country and countrymen. Alas, a few years ago, I should have said, "my universe," but now my mind has been opened to higher views of things.

Place a penny on the middle of one of your tables in space; and leaning over it, look down upon it. It will appear a circle. But now, drawing back to the edge of the table, gradually lower your eye (thus bringing yourself more and more into the condition of the inhabitants of *Flatland*), and you will find the penny becoming more and more oval to your view, and at last when you have placed your eye exactly on the edge of the table (so that you are, as it were, actually a Flatlander), the penny will then have ceased to appear oval at all, and will have become, so far as you can see, a straight line.

The story goes on to discuss the events surrounding the arrival of a visitor from Spaceland, a three-dimensional universe not unlike our own world. A Square's struggle as a 2-D being trying to relate to a 3-D alien mirrors exactly what we feel when trying to understand unseen or unknowable dimensions. Note the following exchange, as the visitor speaks to A Square and tries to prove his third-dimensional nature:

> The diminished brightness of your eye indicates incredulity. But now prepare to receive proof positive of the truth of my assertions. You cannot indeed see more than one of my sections, or Circles, at a time; for you have no power to raise your eye out of the plane of Flatland; but you can at least see that, as I rise in Space, so my sections become smaller. See now, I will rise; and the effect upon your eye will be that my Circle will become smaller and smaller till it dwindles to a point and finally vanishes.

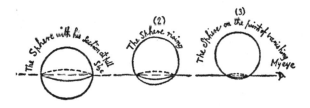

> There was no "rising" that I could see; but he diminished and finally vanished. I winked once or twice to make sure that I was not dreaming. But it was no dream. For from the depths of nowhere came forth a hollow voice—close to my heart it seemed—"Am I quite gone? Are you convinced now? Well, now I will gradually return to Flatland and you shall see my section become larger and larger.

Poor A Square is deemed mad when he tries to tell others what he has learned about Spaceland. He is persecuted and imprisoned, struggling throughout his life to understand and transmit his understanding to his children.

Now ask yourself, "How would *we* do? What if a higher dimensional being came into our space? Would we not see this being as our perceptions in space are trained? Indeed, how could higher dimensional beings relate to us unless they presented themselves in a way we can perceive? File these questions away for a bit. We will get back to them.

To summarize our conclusions thus far:

- Reality is what we perceive and measure.

- Understanding the nature of dimensions is the key to understanding the universe.

- We are limited by our ability to relate in the fixed dimensions of our reality.

In talking about the big bang, we introduced the discovery that the entire universe was expanding as if running away from an explosion in the distant past. The expansion data comes from the measurement of the redshift of the spectra of distant galaxies and objects. This redshift occurs when an object is moving away from the observer at a very high rate of speed. You have experienced this effect whenever an ambulance or fire engine goes by you with its siren screaming. As it approaches, you hear one pitch, as it passes the frequency drops, and you hear yet a third pitch as it speeds away. This is known as the Doppler effect, the principle behind Doppler weather radar! The sound waves bunch up as the source moves toward you and then spread out as it moves away from you. In light spectra, the waves would shift to the blue if an object approaches and shift to the red if it moves away. Edwin Hubble discovered that everything in the sky was redshifted proved that the universe must have started from a single point, followed by an unimaginable explosion.

Every observable object outside the galaxy is running away from every other object. Think about this for a moment: The farther away the object is, the faster it is going, and thus the higher the redshift. Do you find it odd that nothing is coming toward us?

This expansion always brings a thinking person to the same question, "What is the universe expanding into?" Good question!

Now think again of A Square in *Flatland* trying to make sense out of a sphere that seems to move up and down and even disappear altogether. Your struggle in thinking about where the universe expands into is the same perceptual difficulty experienced by A Square.

Now visualize our entire three-dimensional universe confined to the surface of a sphere, with all the galaxies (and space itself) glued to this surface. What would happen if the radius of the surface were to expand? Imagine a balloon with ink spots on the surface. As you blow up the balloon, each spot appears to move away from every other spot on the balloon. More interestingly, the farthest spots seem to be moving away at the greatest speed!

As the radius of the balloon increases, the surface area expands. If this surface area represents the spatial dimensions of the universe, then space itself would be changing size. Thus, the universe is not expanding into anything. The distance between points is growing due to the expansion of space itself.

In the early moments of the universe, the so-called "inflationary period," space actually expanded faster than the speed of light! Since matter was not moving at superlight velocity, this did not violate the speed limits in special relativity. Simply put, space itself is changing size!

Do you feel a headache coming on?

Just as the Flatlander struggles with the third dimension, we struggle with understanding the spatial dimension into which the universe is expanding. For the sake of our visualization, this is one of the higher spatial dimensions. The balloon model explains all the observations. What is even more exciting, the fact that the balloon is growing at a faster and faster rate offers proof that the expansion of the universe is increasing.

Yet another great question to ponder: "Who, or what, is blowing up the balloon?"

The balloon model also removes geocentricity from the big bang. If we picture the explosion in three-dimensional space, every object would appear to be moving away from humans on Earth. If we were to run the movie backward, would that mean we are at the center of the original explosion? This conclusion would have pleased the early church, but, alas, it is flawed. When you look at the balloon surface as if you were an observer on every single spot, you would see that every other dot is moving away from you! Thus there is no special reference frame in the universe.

Hopefully this last point has ended any tendency to look down on the poor Flatlanders as failures in visualizing our dimensional framework. It is just as hard for us to get our minds around the balloon.

By now you may be asking yourself why we have not yet discussed time. We all know that a fourth metric is necessary to describe reality. It is called time, the fourth dimension. Time is different from the other three dimensions. Locating something in space-time requires four numbers (x, y, z, and time). Yet time seems to be fixed, allowing little freedom of motion.

When you make an appointment with someone, you might say, "Meet me at Main and Liberty at 3:00 p.m." Without a time coordinate, you could be at the right place at the wrong time! Even 3:00 p.m. is too ambiguous. It does not take into account someone arriving from a different time zone, say from Houston in Central Standard Time.

Unless you specify Eastern Standard Time where you live, the person may arrive one hour late.

Time is special. It seems to move in only one direction, from past to future. No motion in time seems to be under our control. Time appears to have only one speed, which in fact is not true. That will become clear when we discuss relativity.

It is hard to define time without resorting to time-related parts of speech.

My favorite definition is: "Time is what keeps everything from happening at once!"

When you look at our universe from the perspective of dimensions, we *seem to have* all we need to describe and order our reality. As always, things are both more complex and simultaneously simpler than we think.

Physicists have long been troubled by the nature of time, especially by the so-called "Arrow of Time." While it is clear that time marches in one direction, the universe does not favor any particular direction for the flow of time. Physicists and mathematicians can run all process forward and backward by using spatial descriptors applied to the nonspatial concept of time. It is we, the residents of space-time, who perceive that time runs only in one direction. Our perceptions tell us that we are born, age, and die. The past is behind us and the future has not yet arrived.

Each frame of a motion picture film represents a small fraction of time, actually a still photograph representing a specific moment. When played by the projector in the right sequence, the action moves forward in the same way we perceive normal time. Yet, what happens when we play the film backward? Then the hero can rise from the dead, get younger each day, forget everything that he knew, become a child again, and crawl back into his mother's womb.

Has anyone made a colossal blunder and not wished for a rewind button on the tape? While we cannot do this in the real world, doing so in space-time is not impossible. Physics allows for time to go backward! The trajectory of a thrown ball is still correct with a negative time arrow, as are all the other equations governing motion.

Thus, we can see that universe does not favor any direction in the Arrow of Time.

Why do humans live that way?

At this point in our journey, we have come to terms with cosmology, the big bang, and much of classical physics. This comprises the science by which we were able to organize our observable environment and figure out how things work in our every day lives.

The great challenges that came from extending our success to the very small and the very big were not even realized at the beginning of the twentieth century. The scientific establishment of that time was so arrogant as to state, "We now know everything about everything. The role of scientists in the twentieth century will only be to make better measurements."

Arrogance is always rewarded with disappointment.

To the world of science, it came suddenly, in 1905, from a lowly patent clerk in Bern, Switzerland.

The Music of Creation—Bring in the Strings!

If mathematics is the language of God, then string theory is the music. Once we accept that reality is a perceptual construct, heavily dependent on our ability to sense and measure, we become open to letting the mathematics show us the beauty of creation. It also will lead us into areas of thought that seem as far outside of our everyday world as the third dimension was to the Flatlanders.

For starters, everything you learned in school about atoms was wrong.

The concept of trying to understand nature by breaking it into its smallest components is rooted in ancient Greece. The Greeks conducted thought experiments by chopping matter into smaller and smaller pieces until you could chop no more. This gave rise to the idea of a tiny irreducible, elementary particle called an atom.

For thousands of years science was dominated by Greek concepts. After the Copernican Revolution in astronomy, a new view of the atom emerged. The *formerly irreducible* atom was actually made up of components called protons, neutrons, and electrons that were more elementary than the atom itself.

The classical model of an atom looked a lot like the model of the solar system because it was based on an extension of that same thought process. Where the planets in the solar system were held in their orbits by the pull of the Sun's gravity, electrons were held in their orbits by the attraction of their negative charges to the plus charges of the nucleus. This used the same forms of mathematics. It had a certain beauty. The nucleus was thought to hold protons and neutrons in a small clump in the center, while the electrons were tiny objects orbiting the nucleus like the Earth orbits the Sun.

All of chemistry was based upon this model: elements of the periodic table differed in numbers of protons; isotopes of those elements had different numbers of neutrons; and electrons were arranged in highly ordered, numbered shells. By sharing electrons, chemical reactions produced compounds that make up the myriad structures in the world.

All was well until physicists asked a few silly questions.

According to the model, the nucleus of the atom was composed of positively charged protons compressed into a small, dense central structure that was peppered with neutral particles of similar mass called neutrons. When physicists looked at this, they came across a puzzling fact. Positive charges repel each other with a force equal to the product of the charges divided by the square of the distance between them. Thus, protons in near proximity to each other would be pushed apart with great force. In fact, at the distances in the tiny nucleus, the force would be extremely large.

First silly question: "How can the nucleus of an atom hold itself together?"

The other annoying fact was that opposite charges attract. The orbiting electron with its negative charge would be attracted to the positive charge of the protons in the nucleus. That would cause the electron to acclerate and quickly spiral into the proton. At that point, the electron's negative charge would cancel the proton's positive charge and turn it into a neutron!

Contrary to the chemists' beautiful (and very successful) model, physicists proposed that the nucleus was unstable and would fly apart as its positively charged protons pushed each other out of the way. Thus, there could be no nuclei in the universe!

The electrons of all the atoms in the universe should have spiraled into the nuclei of the atoms, neutralized the protons, and dissolved all matter into a sea of neutrons. As we have observed, these proposals have never occurred. If they had, the history of the universe would have been quite short with no physicists or chemists at all. Since the universe did not die due to these two catastrophes, scientists have continued asking questions according to the scientific model.

When reality is not served by the structure of the model, we change the model to match reality. As it turned out, physicists came up with theories to save the day and allow chemists to keep working.

The first theory was quite obvious. Since the protons in the nucleus are pushing each other away with an incredible amount of force and the nucleus does not fly apart, there must be an opposing force, even stronger than the electrostatic repulsion, which holds the nucleus together.

Physicists have a clever name for this very strong force. We call it *the strong force*.

As to the spiraling electron, we developed the quantum theory, which changed the nature of the electron. Rather than a point particle, it is a wave that could travel only in orbits that were an integer multiple of the electron's wavelength. We will talk more about this later.

When radioactivity was discovered, physicists again had to come up with a new mechanism to explain the decay of nuclear particle/waves and the subsequent release of energy particles. We named the force behind radioactive decay *the weak force*.

Clever, don't you think!

By the early twentieth century, we were left with four fundamental forces that described everything about how the universe worked. They were the force of gravity, the electromagnetic force, the strong force, and the weak force.

Physicists look for simplicity. Thinkers like Einstein wondered why there were four forces and whether or not it was possible to write one theory that would connect all four, a mathematical framework from which one could derive all the properties observed. His failed quest for the unified field theory was presented in the previous chapter.

While there were only four forces governing the framework of the universe, the elementary particle business was booming. With the construction of massive particle accelerators like *Conseil Européen pour la Recherche Nucléaire* (CERN) in Switzerland and Fermilab in Illinois, scientists pressed hard against the limits of the definition. These giant machines accelerated particles to near light speeds, giving them energies that mimic those close to the big bang event itself, and are then smashed into each other.

As the experiments progressed, more and more new particles were discovered. Rather than converging toward simplicity, the models were diverging toward chaos. The great theoretical physicists of the time worried about the fundamental correctness of the model itself.

Richard Feynman argued that we were trying to understand the workings of a fine Swiss watch by smashing it with a sledgehammer and studying the debris.

Was the direction wrong? Should we have been looking for a theoretical framework that would describe all the observed particles as a result of properties of the model?

Of course we should have.

And so we did.

Then a theoretical physicist named Murray Gell-Mann had a mathematical idea. He proposed that the high-energy shattering and resulting new particles could be explained by assuming the existence of a small number of objects known as quarks.

The word quark comes from James Joyce's *Finnegans Wake*, which betrays the whimsical side of the physicist's mind:

> Three quarks for Muster Mark!
> Sure he hasn't got much of a bark
> And sure any he has it's all beside the mark.

An article about quarks in "Projects in Scientific Computing" (2002) portrays the discovery as follows:

> In 1963, theoretical physicist Murray Gell-Mann needed a name for his idea for the building blocks of protons, neutrons and related subatomic particles, till then thought to be indivisible. He settled on quark, a word that combines a dog's bark with a sea gull's squawk and that in German means curd, the fundamental constituent of cheese. Gell-Mann's quarks, which originated as a mathematical glimmer in his mind, have since been substantiated

in many experiments, though no one—for reasons inherent in the nature of quarks—has yet tasted, touched, seen or in any way directly observed one.

The model named six different kinds of quarks with a property known as flavor.

Flavor	Mass (GeV/c^2)	Electric Charge (e)
up (u)	0.004	+2/3
down (d)	0.008	-1/3
charm (c)	1.5	+2/3
strange (s)	0.15	-1/3
top (t)	176	+2/3
bottom (b)	4.7	-1/3

No one has ever seen a quark, yet the assembly of groupings of three different quarks can describe the fundamental three particles quite elegantly.

Put simply, if you take two "up" quarks and one "down" quark, the assembly is a proton. You may remember from high school that chemistry and physics have an electric charge of +1 and a mass of 0.938 GEV/c^2.

The neutron is an assembly of one "up" quark and two "down" quarks. Its mass is 0.940 GEV/c^2 and its charge is zero. Notice the small discrepancy in the mass number between the proton and the neutron.

If you took a neutron and flipped a "down" quark into an "up" quark, it would decay into a proton. The flipping of the quark would result in the release of some energy and a very small particle with a negative charge. The particle emitted is the electron, which has a charge of -1 and a mass small enough to make up most the difference in the mass between the proton and the neutron.

Both theoreticians and experimentalists were quickly won over by the powerful simplicity and elegance of the quark theory to explain observed elementary particles and behaviors.

Conclusion: The large number of particles observed in the accelerator collisions could be easily explained by the existence of a very small number of *flavored* and *colored* quarks.

Beauty, elegance, and symmetry were restored to the universe.

In the later part of the twentieth century, a new theory arose that was a direct descendant of the quark theory and the work that ensued. It was called string theory. In string theory, even the quarks are defined as representations of one two new fundamental building blocks known as "strings."

Strings!

You might ask, "Strings of what?"

Imagine small (very, very small) pieces of space-time, moving about in what we call reality. These strings can be closed, like loops, or open, like a hair. Based on whether it is closed or open, as a string moves through time, it traces out a tube or a sheet.

The sheets and loops are membranes and are also either open or closed. Furthermore, the string is free to vibrate. Since different modes are seen as different masses or spins, different vibration modes represent all the different particle types.

As a mathematical and geometric model, string theory succeeded in reducing the complexity of what we observed in nature.

I will spare you the mathematics, which are not easy and way beyond the scope of this book. However, consider that string theory has been described as a *twenty-first century theory* that was *delivered in the twentieth century*.

Any reader who wants to learn more about string theory would do well to read *The Elegant Universe* by Brian Greene. He is a fellow graduate of my alma mater, Stuyvesant High School. The book became a breakthrough best seller a few years ago and consequently launched a *Nova* series on PBS. The self-proclaimed name for this new set of ideas is "The Theory of Everything."

If that sounds arrogant, ponder this. The mathematics underlying string theory demand the inclusion of additional dimensions for the universe. The solutions propose that the universe is composed of many more dimensions that lie outside of our awareness. In fact, based on the current version of the theory, the universe is composed of ten or eleven spatial dimensions!

Since we can see and measure only three, where are the others?

The theory also suggests that the other six or seven dimensions collapsed into points at the big bang in an infinitesimally short time after time began. These dimensions are curled up so tightly that we cannot perform any measurements to detect their existence, and yet the mathematics demand that they are there.

If string theory is to describe a theory of everything, it is very helpful to have these so-called "compact dimensions." We depend on them for a description of reality based on the prediction of the mathematics and the observations we can make of the behavior of matter in the three dimensions. Some theorists suggest that the contraction of these other dimensions must have provided the tremendous energy that drove the rapid expansion of the universe during the "inflationary" phase of the creation. Before this model, scientists could not explain how the universe could expand so quickly based on the energy they measured. The contraction of the super dimensions would have yielded more than enough power for the expansion of the three spatial dimensions that remained.

If you recall our earlier discussion, the universe expanded at a speed greater than the speed of light during the inflationary phase. This did not violate the special relativity speed of light limit since it was space itself that expanded rather than the matter within it. The very metric of space was expanding at an almost inconceivable rate.

What should we take away from this discussion?

First, our understanding of matter as tangible and real is flawed. The objects that we sense as matter are composed of things as ephemeral as vibrating strings of space-time constructs.

Second, the structure of physical matter is made up of a relatively small number of components that are not observable or measurable. The fact that one could turn a proton into a neuron (or vice versa) by merely flipping an up quark into a down quark is incredible.

What is more incredible is that all of creation can be constructed (and morphed into anything else) from only a few components. The exercise in reductionism begun by the Greeks is almost complete.

While people like Einstein and Hawking wonder what God was thinking at the creation, younger scientists have discovered the Lego building blocks that he was using. As the next few centuries pass, we may be able to manipulate matter and energy at a level that would make the holy grail of alchemy (turning lead into gold) look like child's play.

Consider what the grand unification of the four forces and the theory of everything will give us.

We will be able to create and destroy matter at will.

Utilizing antigravity technologies, we will be able to lift entire cities into space. By removing inertia from its mass, we will be able to accelerate these space-traveling cities to near the speed of light using about as much energy as hitting a golf ball.

Perhaps we won't need to bother with space travel at all if we learn how to open wormholes to any place (or time) in the universe.

It may even be possible to extract energy from the folded-up dimensions, giving us unlimited clean energy.

Science fiction?

Not really.

These speculations are based on the implications of solving these fundamental concepts. They are out of our reach today only because we are not yet done with our studies.

Can we accept that reality is more than we can perceive? That there are more dimensions than we know of? Is all the time and space that we do perceive a derivative of a process that cannot be understood without some component of faith?

As science marches on, we must identify the goal. Otherwise, how could we agree that we have achieved it?

We, the children of God, will have almost all the powers of God.

But will we have the wisdom to control that power and utilize it for the greater good?

Or will our darker side prevail?

The Lord's prayer says, "Thy will be done on Earth, as it is in Heaven." In the next few centuries, science will take us closer to the mind of God. Yet history has shown that we have not yet learned how to be like God in terms of following the guidelines offered by the teachings and writings of our great religions.

J. Robert Oppenheimer was the great physicist who led the Manhattan Project to build the first atomic bomb. When he witnessed the detonation of the Trinity device at Los Alamos, he is quoted as thinking:

> We knew the world would not be the same. A few people laughed, a few people cried, most people were silent. I remembered the line from the Hindu scripture, the Bhagavad-Gita. Vishnu, who is trying to persuade the Prince that he should do his duty and impress him takes on his multi-armed form and says, "Now, I am become Death, the destroyer of worlds." I suppose we all thought that one way or another. (James A. Hijiya, *The Gita of Robert J. Oppenheimer*. Proceedings of the American Philosophical Society, 144:2. June 2000).

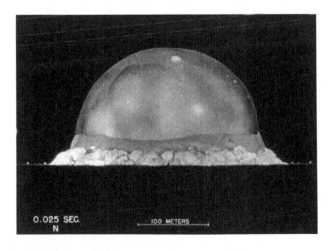

0.025 SEC.
N
100 METERS

Science will give us the power to be gods.

Will we live up to the responsibility? Will we be able to control and manage such power?

Will we survive as a race?

Only God knows.

And only God can help us with the challenges ahead.

From a Quantum Cat to Predestination and Free Will

Our final voyage through modern physics brings us to quantum mechanics. Just as string theory uses mathematics to extend our understanding beyond our limited ability to sense how the universe works, QM takes us down a series of logical paths and truths to places that seem like Alice's wonderland.

The world before quantum mechanics was easier to understand. Physicists built upon a mechanistic, deterministic framework and believed that their understanding of the universe was nearly complete. Their arrogance belied the anomalies in a number of observations and experiments, and all seemed calm.

Indeed, the great confidence generated by the mathematics and mechanics of Newton and his colleagues has a strong basis in the predictive power of science at the beginning of the twentieth century. Physicists stated as a foundational principle that the future state of the universe could be predicted if we knew all the current states and had enough calculative power. Thus, it could be posed, the future would be fixed, and all motion and energy transformation predetermined. In reality, we simply do not have enough math or knowledge to accurately predict the future.

In theology, the concept of predestination has deep roots and important philosophical impact. If the future is inevitable, then why does God hold man accountable for his actions? Unless we can affect events and actions in times to come, what is the point of doing anything? If God already knows how it will all turn out, why bother to be good?

Newton's deterministic universe implied that the creator built it and set it into motion at the creation. Then all subsequent events resulted from the unfolding of all matter following the laws of physics.

Physicists' view of a deterministic universe crumbled with the arrival of a new field of study known as quantum mechanics. The study of QM is complex, but its roots come from the brilliant thought experiments of a group of young scientists in the early 1900s, including Albert Einstein, Max Planck, and Niels Bohr.

Awarded the Nobel Prize in 1921, Einstein's great contribution to science was his 1905 paper on the photoelectric effect. At the time, scientists were trying to interpret the results of experiments when metallic surfaces were hit by light of various frequencies. In some cases, electric currents were induced in the metal. What was odd was the observation of a threshold frequency at which the current began.

If light was composed of electromagnetic waves, and thus contained energy, one would expect the current to be proportional to the intensity of the waves. Thus, higher intensity should mean more energy and thus more current. Below the threshold frequency, there was no current at any intensity, which showed that the model of energy transfer was flawed. At the threshold frequency, even at low intensity, there was a current, and increasing the intensity of the light did increase the amount of current flowing.

Another interesting observation came from an experiment concerning the spectra emitted from materials heated to incandescence (the black body experiment). In 1900, Max Planck proposed that oscillating atoms absorb and emit energy only in discrete bundles (called quanta) rather than continuously as assumed in classical physics. The energy at which the heated element is allowed to emit quanta is the product of its frequency and a new constant, which Planck named Planck's constant.

Einstein solved the puzzle of the photoelectric effect by proposing that light was made up of particles of energy, photons, with the size of the energy being related to the frequency of the photon using exactly the same formula as Planck. These discrete particles of light were quanta of energy. When it strikes an electron in the metal with sufficient energy, the free electron is kicked out of its atomic shell and becomes current. Since energy can be absorbed only in discrete quanta units, no number lower than threshold frequency quanta can kick the electron out. With simple mathematics, Einstein changed our view of light and energy from continuous to discrete, which formed the basis of what would later become quantum mechanics.

Rather than being made up of particles, matter seemed to behave like waves. This struck old science like a tsunami. After hundreds of years of incremental progress, here was a giant discontinuity that appeared to be ridiculous, but was verifiable by experiments that were repeatable and predictive.

As we discussed in the previous chapter, the model of the classical atom no longer fit reality. Bohr realized that a catastrophic implosion was avertable if one constructed a model in which the electrons were required to orbit in fixed radii. The size of these orbits would be related to the radius at which a whole number of wavelengths could fit on the circumference of the orbit. The electron is thus not acting as a particle (like a planet), but is instead a wave of fixed length.

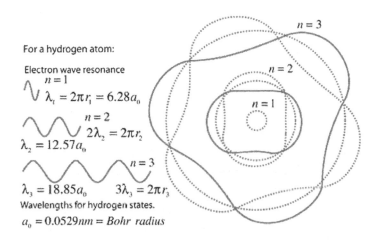

For a hydrogen atom:

Electron wave resonance

$n = 1$

$\lambda_1 = 2\pi r_1 = 6.28 a_0$

$n = 2$

$2\lambda_2 = 2\pi r_2$

$\lambda_2 = 12.57 a_0$

$n = 3$

$\lambda_3 = 18.85 a_0 \qquad 3\lambda_3 = 2\pi r_3$

Wavelengths for hydrogen states.

$a_0 = 0.0529 nm = Bohr\ radius$

Imagine if you will a violin string. Since it is fixed at both ends, there are only a few waves that can fit on the string. One wavelength, two, three, and so on. If you make the string into a loop, then only integer numbers of waves can fit on the loop. (Just as the note model occurs in string theory). Therefore, there are only a small set of *allowed* orbits for an electron in an atom.

Interestingly, an electron is capable of *leaping* from a lower orbit to a higher one by absorbing a specific amount of energy. When it falls back to a lower orbit, it does so by emitting this same amount of energy in a specific object called a quantum of energy, which is a photon. This jumping from orbit to orbit is what is known as a quantum leap.

Two results are immediate: First, this model averts the spiral catastrophe problem of the classical atom; and second, it explains why different elements, when heated, give off light in specific discrete spectral lines. Today's chemistry is the basis of much of modern technology.

To summarize, the quantum model of the atom proves that electrons are waves and particles, which we describe as the dual nature of matter. It undermines the idea of fixed particles as things as derived by the thought processes used by the Greeks thousands of years ago.

Even more amazing is the fact that an electron jumps from one orbit to the other without ever being in the middle! What does that mean? Think of the transporter on Star Trek. You step in at one place and are instantaneously beamed to another place. As far out as matter transporters may seem, every electron in the universe does it every day.

Scientists today are pondering instantaneous transportation via less painful methods than those used on Star Trek, such as wormholes and something called quantum entanglement. Tune in later in the century for the latest developments.

Hopefully, you're beginning to grasp how powerfully quantum mechanics alters our view of matter. Let's discuss one more major experiment called the double-slit interference experiment. This is quite easy to understand and is often performed with water waves in high school physics class.

When a water wave passes through a single slit it makes the pattern shown below:

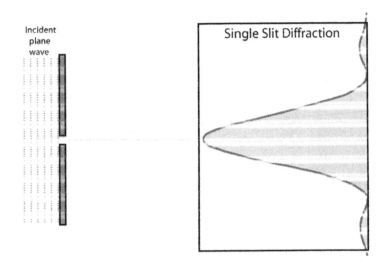

When the wave passes through two slits, the waves produced at the slits interfere with each other and form what we clever scientists call an interference pattern.

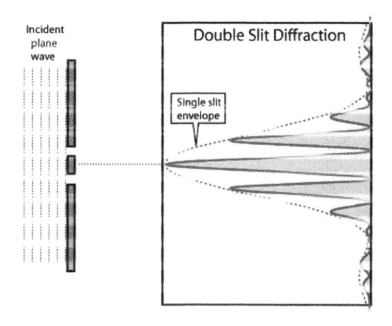

Doing the same experiment with light yields the same result. With light going through two slits, you see characteristic dark bands interspersed with bright ones. This is classical wave behavior.

When the experiment is done with electrons, the single-slit and double-slit runs behave exactly as the two runs with water and light. The dual nature of electrons implies that it behaves like a wave when it passes through the slit, which allows us to measure its location on the screen, as a particle. The state of the second slit seems to affect the behavior and trajectory of the electron. But how does the electron as a particle wave at the left slit know if the right slit is opened or closed?

What enters the scientific picture at this point is the concept of probability. It turns out that the behavior of the electron is governed by the Schrödinger wave equation which considers the *probability* of the particle's location and energy. The electron has a probability of being in various places in the future. When one event actually occurs, all the other probability functions collapse to zero since they did not happen.

Newton's deterministic universe crumbled. QM gives us a world in which probability determines outcomes.

Einstein hated this idea. He is often quoted as saying, "God does not play dice with the Universe!" He considered QM to be flawed for this reason.

Schrödinger's Cat

The argument is often summed up by a discussion of Schrödinger's cat. Schrödinger proposed that you place a cat into a box with a bottle of poison with a trigger controlled by a random timer switch. This implies that the bottle will open and kill the cat at some time that you don't know. The question asked some later time: "Is the cat dead or alive?"

According to Einstein, it is either one or the other, which we cannot know until we open the box. Schrödinger says that it is neither. Rather the cat is a mixture of dead and alive and only becomes one or the other when we open the box.

Stated in a different way, there is a 50 percent probability that the cat is alive, and a 50 percent probability that he is dead. You cannot know until you open the box because it is the act of observing that makes one of the probabilities go to 100 percent while the other drops to zero.

Try to wrap your head around this. The cat is both alive and dead until we open the box and see one outcome as real. The very act of observing effects which reality occurs. As we introduced earlier, the observer is an essential force in determining the path of reality!

Here is a great tidbit to use at a cocktail party. If a tree falls in the forest and there is no one to hear it, does it make a sound? Based upon our understanding of QM, the answer is no! Not only is there no sound but also it could be argued that there might not even be a tree!

However, what if the tree falls on a power line and causes an outage at my house? I can work backward from this observation to find the cause of the power disruption, thus proving that a tree fell in the forest. I still am incapable of saying that it made a sound!

The universe is a strange place when viewed from the quantum mechanical mindset. Determinism is replaced by probability, and reality becomes dependent upon observers and measurement. Nothing actually occurs unless it is measured, and the act of observing determines the outcome of each probabilistic event. The universe actually requires observers! Grasping this concept will become important in our quest for understanding our roles in the universe.

The fundamental concept that the outcomes of an event each carry a probability until it is observed or measured is at the root of how quantum mechanics views the world. Stated differently, for every option (choice), there are multiple possible outcomes. Each outcome has a probability. When a measurement occurs (a choice is made), all other probabilities drop to zero. The chosen outcome's probability went to 100 percent.

This has profound implications when applied to really important scenarios, like your life.

Your life is the result of an infinitely complex series of choices. Think about it. Where you are right now is the result of each choice you made in the past.

For example, you decided to go to the party where you met your spouse. You also decided not to cheat on the big exam, which led to your getting a bad grade that prevented you from getting into medical school.

You get the idea.

Choices.

Outcomes.

Consequences.

Theologically, you had free will to make each choice. Thus, it could be argued that your version of reality was created by you!

If you map someone's sequence of decision points, each results in a different reality:

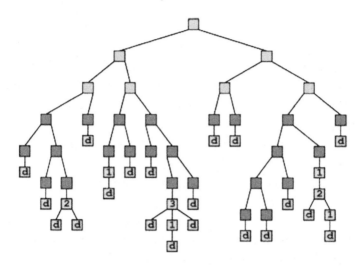

Schrödinger's cat was both alive and dead until the box was opened. At that point, the universe split into two realities: one in which the cat is alive and another in which it is dead. Both are equally real—but you (your consciousness) can only be in one or the other! Each series of outcomes traces a unique path in space-time called a time line. Each path is real to the observers in that path.

This idea implies the existence of a real universe in which Lee Harvey Oswald missed JFK, one in which the Black Death wiped out all Europe, and another in which Martin Luther King survived his assassination attempt and became president of the United States. In some universes, Germany developed the atomic bomb first and won the war.

More personally, imagine a universe in which your parents never met, which means you do not exist. Or one in which you did cheat on the exam, became a great doctor, and discovered the cure for cancer.

Hopefully, you get the idea, and perhaps another headache!

Let's talk more about time travel. As a mainstay of science fiction in both literature and film, we have always enjoyed a good time travel paradox. For example, if you were to build a time machine and go back to your grandfather's childhood, and caused an accident in which he is killed, what happens? The paradox is that if your grandfather is killed as a child, he never marries your grandmother, one of your parents is never born, and thus you were never born. If you were never born, how could you build the time machine to go back and cause the death of your grandfather as a child?

We have free will to make choices, each leading to a different reality and cutting off all other realities. We perceive time as moving from one choice to another so that our lives assume a single time line in space-time. It is plausible to say that the passing of time is required for events to occur.

Let's return to our discussion about predestination. We asked the question, "If we had no choice, why have rules and punishment?" The truth is that we do have the freedom to choose outcomes. We do have free will and can be held responsible and accountable.

Here is the mind bender.

According to the QM model, every outcome of every choice exists in the quantum multiverse. God is outside of time. To Him the quantum multiverse is stateless and changeless since change is related to time. Since God is outside time, all futures already exist! Thus, all outcomes can be said to be predetermined and known to an observer at a higher dimension. Free will is the choice we make in each second *inside of time* because we live in time.

We have the power to choose our path through space-time. According to a standard of morality, we can be *good* or *bad*. We can follow the rules or break them. It is up to each of us to make the reality that we live.

God gave us a user's manual as distilled in the Ten Commandments. Imagine what the world would be like if everyone followed these ten simple rules.

I have always found it fascinating that civilized beings have raised the complexity of rules to the point where the law is more difficult than quantum electrodynamics! Yet the world still deals with simple concepts like evil, greed, murder, and theft.

Ten simple rules. You can create your reality by making good decisions every day.

Free will.

What a concept!

What a responsibility.

When I first heard the prayer "Our Father, who art in heaven," I was struck by the phrase "Thy will be done on Earth as it is in Heaven." I saw a profound message in these words. If we did follow the religious rules of the Hebrews and the teachings of Christ, if we acted in the ways that the Old and New Testaments encourage us to act, our lives on Earth would be more like the unimaginable perfection of heaven.

Think of it. We will grow in intellectual power and learn to control the fundamental forces in the universe to do our bidding. Sometime soon we will have the power to extend life, and perhaps even to create it.

But without a sound foundational infrastructure of ethics and a true and honest commitment to good, all this power will likely lead to the destruction of our race or even our planet. We will make the reality, and it will be either a heaven or hell.

We have the freedom to choose. Will we have the maturity and wisdom to choose well?

God has given us minds, souls, and free will. Only He knows what we will do with his spectacular and beautiful creation.

How Can Scientists Believe that God Exists?

> I want to know how God created this world. I am not interested in this or that phenomenon, in the spectrum of this or that element. I want to know His thoughts; the rest are details.
>
> —Albert Einstein, United States (German-born) physicist (1879–1955)

Einstein is not questioning the existence of God. He is stating his belief in God, his belief in the fact that God created this world. Einstein wished to know the thoughts of God!

Do these statements sound like the words of someone who does not believe that God exists? Indeed, how can they not believe?

As the theory of the big bang emerged, it challenged a fundamental canon of science, that every event can be explained in a continuous, rational manner from every previous event. Simply put, every effect must have a cause. Thus, there cannot be a first cause. Arno Penzias, the Nobel Prize winner for discovering the big bang background radiation, wrote: "Astronomy leads us to a unique event, a universe which was created out of nothing and delicately balanced to provide exactly the conditions required to support life. In the absence of an absurdly-improbable accident, the observations of modern science seem to suggest an underlying, one might say, supernatural plan" (Walter Bradley, "The 'Just So' Universe: The Fine-Tuning of Constants and Conditions in the Cosmos," in William Dembski and James Kushiner, eds., *Signs of Intelligence*, 168).

Many scientists rebelled at such a thought. Arthur Eddington, one of the giants of twentieth century physics, said of the big bang model in 1931: "The notion of a beginning is repugnant to me...I simply do not believe that the present order of things started off with a bang...the expanding Universe is preposterous...incredible...it leaves me cold."

Phillip Morrison of Massachusetts Institute of Technology (MIT) stated on a BBC Documentary: "I find it hard to accept the big bang theory; I would like to reject it."

Even Allan Sandage, one of the astronomers at Palomar Observatory who verified the expansion of the universe, expressed his doubt: "It is such a strange conclusion...it cannot really be true."

Note that these are all emotional responses. As the evidence for a beginning mounted, the old steady state model in which the universe had always existed lost footing and withered as all unsupported science should.

And yet here was the big bang, all but screaming at scientists through the background radiation and the uniform expansion of the universe—measurable, verifiable evidence that the universe had a beginning.

The wall separating science from theology quickly began to tumble.

In *The Beginning and End of the World* (Riddell Memorial Lectures, Fourteenth Series, Oxford, 1942), British physicist Edmund Whitaker wrote: "What came before the beginning? There is no ground for supposing that matter and energy existed before and was suddenly galvanized into action. For what could distinguish that moment from all other moments in eternity? It is simpler to postulate creation ex nihilo—Divine will constituting Nature from nothingness."

In his treatise, *God and the Astronomers* (W. W. Norton, New York, 1978), Robert Jastrow offers a lament typical of many scientists during that time: "Consider the enormity of the problem. Science has proven that the Universe exploded into being at a certain moment. It asks, 'What cause produced this effect? Who or what put the matter and energy into the Universe? Was the Universe created out of nothing, or was it gathered together out of pre-existing materials? And science cannot answer these questions.'"

The big bang obliterated the possibility that we could know anything about *before*. It posted a sign saying that science could go no further in its understanding.

Simply put, the big bang required a first cause and a prime mover.

No alternative analysis can be constructed to match the facts of time and space having a specific moment of beginning.

This precisely explains why many scientists have come to believe that God exists.

A bold statement, yet easily verified. In previous chapters, you have read quotes from great minds and thinkers: Einstein and Hawking, Newton and Feynman. They all talk about God as an agent of creation.

In this brief overview of science and the incredible intellectual construct that it represents, we have learned about the very small and the very big, about the order and the processes of the creation of the universe, the evolution of the stars and planets, and the mystery of life itself. Human minds have come to this knowledge, and the fruit of their labors form the basis of modern civilization.

How can scientists become people of faith? Many people consider science and theology antithetical.

The explanation is very simple.

Scientists are children with open minds. They ask, probe, and analyze. They theorize. They postulate. They demand proof and find it.

But what about things that seem beyond proof?

The scientific approach of honest intellectual query can extend even *beyond the provable*. This knowledge forms the foundation of things that must be true without proof. This implies a level of order and design that make it possible for the human mind to use logic and analysis to find answers without resorting to the use of supernatural powers.

This is why Einstein believed in God. Not the God of the Jews or the Christians, but the God that created the universe and caused the big bang.

Hawking tries to understand the mind of God at that first second by musing whether or not God had any choice in the laws of physics laid down in creation, in the various constraints of nature, or in the laws governing the forces that make the universe what it is.

Note that these scientists do not challenge the existence of God as the creator of the universe. They clearly see him in the fabric of the creation. They discuss God's role, the decision to give human beings freedom of choice, and even his gambling prowess. Einstein said, "God does not play Dice with the Universe." Hawking answered, "Not only does he play dice, but he rolls them where no one can see."

We have noted many signs of God's existence: the beauty and simplicity of mathematics implied by the grand design; the equations describing the four fundamental forces (a constant times the product of specific properties divided by the square of the distance between them); the small numbers of elementary objects; and the musical nature of the strings which seem to be the work of a great unseen artist.

In discussing the time *before* the big bang, I posed that since time itself did not begin until after the creation, the concept of *before* has no meaning. The agent of creation exists outside of time. Since space was created in the big bang, the Creator exists outside the three dimensions that we call space.

Where is God? God exists in a place outside of the space and time in which we live. No other answer is logically consistent with the creation of the universe in a big bang.

Thus, God does not have the same sense of time that we do. In fact, we cannot begin to imagine what God's environment or reality might be like, just as the Flatlanders could not conceive of a universe in which there was a third dimension.

We owe our existence not only to the big bang but also to the granularity of matter in the early universe. Mapping the big bang radiation cloud reveals an interesting mystery.

The Microwave Sky Image from the WMAP Mission

Remember that when we look out into space, we are looking into the *past*. The above is a visual representation of the early universe taken in the microwave spectrum. What is especially meaningful about this picture is that the colors, which represent energy density, are not uniform. Put another way, there are *lumps* in the image.

Without these lumps in the early cloud, galactic clouds would have had no way to form. In fact, there would have been no structures of any kind.

No galaxies, no stars, no planets, no us! Human beings literally would not exist unless the creation had lumps.

Scientists have no model or theory that explains how the lumps formed from a symmetrical process like the big bang. Some offer the *hand of God* as a possible agent. As Genesis says, "And the Spirit of God moved upon the face of the waters."

Until a better model comes along, the mystery of these lumps will continue to puzzle us.

Another remarkable feature of the universe is that it is highly uniform in structure. According to the relativity theory, there should be no causal connection between points separated by distances greater than c multiplied by t (where c is the velocity of light and t is the age of the universe). Translation: The speed of light is a constant and the maximum speed at which information could be transferred.

Thus, the universe is so vast that regions within it are too far away from each other to share information. Regions are so far apart that there has not been enough time in the history of the universe for any transfer of information to have occurred. Thus, there can be no way for information such as universal constants, laws of physics, and the rules of how things work to have been shared.

And yet, these constants, laws, and rules are the same everywhere!

Cosmology suggests that the primordial universe was partitioned into a large number of causally separate regions. Nevertheless, all these disconnected regions had to expand at the same rate to maintain the observed degree of uniformity!

Why is the universe the same everywhere?

Because constants are constant no matter where we look!

How can this be? I invoke another great physicist and author, Paul Davies:

> It is hard to resist the impression of something—some influence capable of transcending space-time and the confinement of relativistic causality—possessing an overview of the entire cosmos at the instant of its creation, and manipulating all the causally disconnected parts to go bang with almost exactly the same vigor at the same time, and yet not so exactly coordinated as to preclude the small scale, slight irregularities that eventually formed the galaxies, and us. (Davies, P, *The Accidental Universe.* Cambridge: Cambridge University Press, 1982. p. 95.)

Is life a miracle that occurred only once in the entire universe, only on Earth? Most scientists think not. Carl Sagan writes about billions and billions of stars, which suggests the sheer magnitude of possible life-bearing worlds just in our own Milky Way.

As a basis to justify the SETI project, the famous Drake equation as defined below: $N = N^* fp\ ne\ fl\ fi\ fc\ fL$. It attempts to calculate the total number of communicating intelligent civilizations by considering a number of questions.

N^* represents the number of stars in the Milky Way galaxy.

Question: How many stars are in the Milky Way galaxy?

Answer: Current estimates are one hundred billion.

fp is the fraction of stars that have planets around them.

Question: What percentage of stars have planetary systems?

Answer: Current estimates range from 20 percent to 50 percent.

ne is the number of planets per star that are capable of sustaining life.

Question: For each star that does have a planetary system, how many planets are capable of sustaining life?

Answer: Current estimates range from one to five.

fl is the fraction of planets in ne where life evolves.

Question: On what percentage of the planets that are capable of sustaining life does life actually evolve?

Answer: Current estimates range from 100 percent (where life can evolve it will) down to close to 0 percent.

fi is the fraction of fl where intelligent life evolves.

Question: On the planets where life does evolve, what percentage evolves intelligent life?

Answer: Estimates range from 100 percent (intelligence is such a survival advantage that it will certainly evolve) down to near 0 percent.

fc is the fraction of fi that communicate.

Question: What percentage of intelligent races have the means and the desire to communicate?

Answer: Ten percent to twenty percent.

fL is fraction of the planet's life during which the communicating civilizations live.

Question: For each civilization that does communicate, for what fraction of the planet's life does the civilization survive?

Answer: This is the toughest of the questions. If we take Earth as an example, the expected lifetime of our Sun and the Earth is roughly ten billion years. So far we've been communicating with radio waves for less than one hundred years. How long will our civilization survive? Will we destroy ourselves in a few years like some predict, or will we overcome our problems and survive for millennia? If we were destroyed tomorrow, the answer to this question would be 1/100,000,000th. If we survive for 10,000 years, the answer will be 1/1,000,000th.

When all of these variables are multiplied together when come up with: *N*, the number of communicating civilizations in the galaxy.

With reasonable assumptions, Drake equation predicts thousands of communicating civilizations. The dark side of SETI is that we have yet to find one. Enrico Fermi reduced the whole SETI project to one negative thought, "If they existed, they would be here."

Yet SETI continues and scientists are still seeking evidence of the existence of extraterrestrial life.

Why does the possibility of life seem to be built into the very fabric of the universe?

Do you recall our discussion about the incredible pervasiveness of carbon, oxygen, hydrogen, and nitrogen (COHN)? Apparently these elements, the precise building blocks of life, exist everywhere in the universe. Scientists have seen organic molecules in the spectra of nebula in distant galaxies. Perhaps within the next twenty years we could discover whether life exists elsewhere in our solar system, and by extension, postulate whether or not we are alone in the universe.

DNA is essentially a computer and factory capable of self replication, which by trial and error can improve itself. DNA also can build so many different life-forms and structures with only *four* components! Scientists expect to find life elsewhere in the universe. We have long since abandoned the concept that we are the center of the universe and God's only creation. We could even discover other kinds of life not based on DNA.

Intelligent design poses that God actually designed the universe and DNA in order to build us. This belief fails to recognize that we are not the endpoint of the process. DNA will continue to improve itself. Will we still be here a million years from now? Or will there be some more advanced form of DNA life (or non-DNA life) pondering the very same questions.

The reality is that we dwell on a single planet in an insignificant solar system on the edge of an arm of an average galaxy. We are the product of an infinite number of events occurring in a specific order. If any one of them had gone another way, we may never have come into being.

All that chaos.

All that catastrophic violence.

And yet you and I are here.

We exist.

Human beings are no less than miracles. So too will be our children's children, one million years from now.

And still we dare to ponder the existence of the entity that created us. We study and analyze God's truly miraculously understandable creation.

In the introduction to Hawking's *A Brief History of Time*, Carl Sagan describes how most people experience life:

> We go about our daily lives understanding almost nothing of the world. We give little thought to the machinery that generates the sunlight that makes life possible, to the gravity that glues us to an Earth

that would otherwise send us spinning off into space, or to the atoms of which we are made and on whose stability we fundamentally depend. Except for children (who don't know enough not to ask the important questions), few of us spend much time wondering why nature is the way it is; where the cosmos came from, or whether it was always here; if time will one day flow backward and effects precede causes; or whether there are ultimate limits to what humans can know.

After all that we have learned, and all that we have yet to learn, we still find miracles. The more we know, the more we learn to respect the creation. We respect the power and beauty of the creation and its primary agent. Let's close with another quote from Jastrow's God and the astronomers: "This is an exceedingly strange development, unexpected by all but the theologians. They have always accepted the word of the Bible: In the beginning God created heaven and earth.... [But] for the scientist who has lived by his faith in the power of reason, the story ends like a bad dream. He has scaled the mountains of ignorance; he is about to conquer the highest peak; [and] as he pulls himself over the final rock, he is greeted by a band of theologians who have been sitting there for centuries."

I believe that scientists and theologians will finally merge their worldviews and help each other to understand the universe from a unified point of view.

Just as God intended from the beginning.

Soul Searching and Searching for the Soul

It's time to explore what may be our strangest mystery—our souls.

With my apologies to my English teachers, I would like to first pose the question, "*What* is Me?"

In the mirror, I see a handsome, middle-aged man, with less hair than I would like and carrying more weight than I should, but still charming and sexy...at least to my wife!

Since my reflection has changed incredibly over the years, can that really be me? I remember a young boy, who looked a lot like my sons. I remember a cocky teenager with a beard and lots of hair. Once upon a time, the mirror showed me an image of a scholarly and dedicated undergraduate, with a smirk betraying my inner love of life. Other images included a young and cocky NASA rocket scientist, an overly serious graduate student, a college professor, a father and husband, and all the while *change was the only constant.*

I know all about what makes up my body, the atoms, molecules, and cells that have been changing throughout my life. Thankfully, the collection of stuff that is my body is still winning the war against the second law of thermodynamics by exporting entropy to the universe. I eat, drink, breathe, and send unused and chemically modified refuse outside of the closed system that is my body.

Since my body is constantly changing, is it reasonable to think that me is my body?

Of course not!

So I ask, "W*here* is Me?"

Am I in my brain? Certainly it stores my memories. I use my brain's processing power to manage input from the world and respond. Drinking too much wine can impair my connection to reality. Disease has the potential of dulling my memory or rendering me unable to see, hear, or think.

Human beings have thought about the concept of a soul for a very long time as perhaps encapsulating the sum total of a person's identity. We accept the fundamental duality of a person taught in most philosophies and religions.

The simple answer to my queries is that I am a composite entity made of a physical body and a not-so-physical soul. I view the soul as my spirit, which theologians say is given to me by God.

This book was born a decade ago in a Sunday school class at the First Presbyterian Church in Kingwood, Texas. I asked the minister, Dr. Robert Covington, when he believed my soul was given to me. His answered, "You pose a most difficult question. The Roman Catholics seem to teach that ensoulment takes place immediately on conception. As Father Borely used to tell me, 'If it is not going to become a human being...what is it going to become...so there!'" St. Augustine and St. Thomas taught that ensoulment takes place when the fetus could breathe outside the womb. Genesis says, "God breathed into Adam and he became a living soul." The Hebrew word is *nefish*, the same word for the "spirit of God moving across the face of the deep." All Abrahamic monotheists agree on such a process.

Thus, we can agree that the soul and the body are two distinct entities that are tied together at the fertilization of an egg, sometime during the pregnancy, or at birth. Souls exist.

But what is this soul, and is it me? Are my memories and personality properties of my soul? If so, where are they stored? If the soul survives the body, do our memories and personalities live on?

Thinkers have tried to identify the location or physicality of the soul for centuries. Some have even weighed bodies as they transitioned from life to death, looking for a measurable decrease in mass. None has ever been found.

Apart from people who have had near-death experiences, no one knows exactly what happens when a person dies. The biochemical machine changes very little from the moment before death to the moment after. Many people have been present when friends and family members draw their last breath. Their hearts stop and brain waves monitored by the EKG flat line. However at the cellular level, bodies that appear dead continue to function normally for a short time. With cessation of circulation and respiration, the system slowly loses its lifelong battle against entropy. As a scientist, I would say that the precise time of death is not measurable.

About twenty-two years ago, my mother was hospitalized and remained in a coma until my brother and I arrived. I was holding her hand at the precise moment of her death. I felt it. At one moment, the body was my mom, and at the next moment she was gone. Within a few seconds, the monitors announced what I had felt.

What does happen at the moment of death? In the Judeo-Christian belief, the soul exits the body and goes somewhere else. Death is not a physical event, at least not a measurable event. Thus, our search for an answer resides in the realm of metaphysics.

Let's back up a bit. If the body is not me, then the soul must be. As a scientist, am I doomed to rely on a mystical, ethereal entity to explain my own existence?

I doggedly continue to look for me. I know that my body is an incredible assembly of awesome complexity. I have a brain that essentially functions like a computer system, a biochemical equivalent of the laptop which I am using to write this book. The laptop executes programs using silicon, substrates, and copper. My brain uses electrical impulses that travel on complex pathways of neurons.

Am I a set of programs running on a computer?

Is my soul an operating system?

The more I think of it, the more I like this analogy. My body is like a laptop, an assembly of processors, storage, input, and output. Yet until the infusion of a soul, the operating system has no identity or capacity to do anything. Once it is, it becomes possible to load content and programs, and learn how to do things. It can remember things. It can make decisions, answer questions, and even create new things.

My laptop can break. If the hard drive fails, it forgets things.

I can get sick, age, and die!

I was born. I received my soul. My body was equipped with an operating system and programs that allowed me to become an intelligent life-form. I figured out how to eat, how to manipulate my environment by crying, and how to move about first on all fours and then on two wobbly legs. I explored and gathered data about my surroundings. In computer speak, I mastered an I/O protocol that allowed me to interface with other life units (i.e., learned how to talk). I built symbolic logic into heuristic analytical protocols that enabled more efficient data input (i.e., learned to read).

My programs ran 24-7, with a nightly maintenance window during which I slept and rested my operating system. My system turned out to be a good one, just a few bugs here and there.

I went from cute to adorable to charming to sexy, learning more and more about other life units that would enable me to create the next generations. Translated: I met girls and figured out the birds and the bees.

But what does it mean that the soul is a program? The soul is not a thing. It is not measurable. You cannot hold it in your hand. You cannot weigh it.

When we say something exists, there are two distinct meanings. I am sitting on a chair. It is an object that exists in a place in space-time, has a duration (it was made in the past and will be destroyed in the future), and is unambiguous in its *is-ness*. *Atlas Shrugged* is a book on my shelf that is unambiguously as real as the chair. But what of the story told in *Atlas Shrugged*? The pages consist of a contrasting chemical pigment on white plant fiber (ink on paper). Yet the story somehow differs from the is-ness of a real object. After reading the book, part of it becomes part of my memory and learning. If I lose the book, the story of *Atlas Shrugged* continues to exist in my mind.

The same is true of a computer program that exists separately from the computer on which it is loaded. Thus, the computer has a different state of existence than the set of codes that make up a program.

My body and soul both exists, but in a different sense.

If my brain is merely a biochemical computer system, might it eventually be possible to build a computer with equal processing and storage capacity? If my body's programming and memory could be transferred to a computer, would I be in the computer? Would I be able to tell if you were able to "Wi-Fi" the computer that is me? Would I have the same access to my senses? If I existed in the computer and my body was walking around, where would it really be me?

Science fiction writers often focus on far-out ideas and turn them into entertaining stories. Richard K. Morgan is the author of two books about the overlap between technology and the soul. *Altered Carbon* and *Broken Angels* are set about five hundred years in the future, when technology has developed the ability to digitize a person's personality and memories. It is stored in a high-density data stack in the base of the brain. When a person dies, the stack can be placed in a new body, re-sleeved. People's new bodies are a complete continuation of the person's existence thus far. The only way to really die (real death) is to have your stack destroyed. If you like science fiction and crime with a film noir bent, you may find these books intriguing.

It's difficult to imagine what might be possible five hundred years down the road. For hundreds of years, human beings have thought about whether the soul exists separately from the physical body. It's not that great a leap think about technology developing the ability to record store every aspect of a human life in a crystal or chip.

Even so, similar philosophical musings would arise in trying to understand the nature of the soul. Is the person's soul in the stack? Or is it merely a copy? If it were a copy, would it know that it was a copy? Would it care?

Are machines able to think? The idea of a sentient machine has been a fundamental theme in science fiction for more than a century. In fact, I am writing these words on the anniversary of the HAL 9000 computer becoming self aware. His eerie announcement is recorded in Arthur C. Clarke's novel and movie *2001: A Space Odyssey*: "I am a HAL nine thousand computer, Production number 3. I became operational at the HAL plant in Urbana, Illinois, on January 12, 1997."

Why do people seem to dismiss the possibility that machines can think and feel?

To keep grappling with this question, computer science has developed an entire field called artificial intelligence. Common wisdom considers this capacity as a simple matter of complexity and random-access memory (RAM). Many think modern computers are not big enough to become self-aware. This will not always be true. Moore's law states that for almost thirty years, processing power is growing at an exponential rate, doubling every eighteen months. Experts believe this will continue for two or three more decades. We used to dream about a computer that could process a billion calculations a second (one gigahertz).

In time, the computer engineers will design a processor that will be fast enough and have access to as much is stored my brain.

Will that computer become self-aware?

Will it have a soul?

We still do not understand the mechanism of the system load. Theology tells us that God Himself infuses the soul into us. That sounds like a process by which our spirits are downloaded into the naked computer system that is our body. The result is intelligent life.

When I die, will my programs cease?

If yes, will this be the end of me?

I believe that our operating system code and programs are divine and enable me to live, learn, feel, and interact with the physical world. My body is real and exists in space-time. A lobotomy or stroke could erase my personality and memories. Will my soul's computer and storage cease to function when I die? Or, is it possible that all the things that make *me* me will continue to exist after my death? When my body is ashes, could God reupload me to the great processor and storage array of heaven?

Of course He could. He is God, for God's sake!

If my computer dies I can reload the operating system and programs into another computer, and all the data would be the same. Yet because my soul exists outside of time and space, it could certainly transcend space and time.

Many of the world's religions believe in life after death. Judeo-Christians believe in a place called heaven where the soul returns to God for eternity. Both Jews and Christians believe in the physical resurrection of the body at some point in the future. In the Jewish faith, an amputated limb is kept and, if possible, buried with the deceased!

Since the body might be long dispersed by time or fire, theologians have debated this concept for centuries. St. Thomas Aquinas argued against the idea of the resurrection of the dead. In accord with logic, God would be unable to resurrect cannibals since atoms in their bodies would be composed of atoms needed for the resurrection of the people they ate!

Actually, my current body today has different atoms than it did a decade ago, so what does resurrection of my body really mean?

Assuming that all the atoms can be reordered, which body will be resurrected? Will it be the old and frail body you had at the time of your death, or the one in which you graduated high school?

I suspect that everyone would choose the one that was younger and stronger!

Where would we put everyone if the people who ever lived came back to life?

I have already proposed that a God who exists outside of space and time would need to become an entity inside of space and time capable of interacting with us in a relationship. It is completely logical and reasonable to believe that God entered our reality by infusing a special soul, like God himself, into a human body. To believe that Christ was the Son of God is a reasonable explanation of this process. Christ called us children of God. Coupled with the belief that God gives each of us a soul (which may be a part of Him), this truth links all of us to God in a very personal way. Genesis says, "God created man and woman in his own image." My soul came from God, and it is because of God that I am me.

Thank you, God!

More questions arise. Is there an unlimited supply of souls or a fixed number? If life exists elsewhere in the universe, is it intelligent? Do aliens have souls? Realizing that time will not be passing in an afterlife, what will I do?

While I do not know the answers to these questions, I will share with you what I believe. As you study the concept in this book, you may realize that a great many others have come to similar conclusions.

Allow me to summarize this chapter. I believe that a duality exists in ,me. I am both a real, physical being, and also a soul that resides in this body for a time. I believe that the soul exists in a different way than the body does. I believe that the soul exists outside of space and time, just as

God does. I believe that it was God who gave me my soul. It is my soul that is me. Even as my body changes over time and eventually ages and dies, my soul (which exists in a different way than my body) will never cease to exist. If and when the technology exists, I believe that it will possible for me to move to a new body, and that my soul (which is me) could continue to exist outside of space and time in a place like heaven.

Perhaps I am right. I may be wrong.

Our journey has brought us to understand the nature of understanding. That resulted in the seeming arrogance of questioning the mind of God. One last step will help us to see that we are more closely bound to the Creator and the creation than we have ever considered.

The Quantum Leap of Faith

By sharing my thoughts and conclusions with you, I have led you on an exploration of both science and theology. We have journeyed to the edges of modern physics, to the beginnings of time and space, and looked for answers to the great questions that have been asked since the awakening of our intellects.

Why am I here?

Where did I come from?

What will happen to me when I die?

We have learned that science and theology converge in answering these core questions, and that each attempts to meet our need to understand. Both scientists and theologians bring to their crafts a hunger for truth and a need for intellectual and spiritual fulfillment. In that search, they are not that different.

Over the last few thousand years, our civilization has come to an interesting plateau. Technology has produced miracles by the measure of our ancestors. We stand at the beginning of the twenty-first century with enough knowledge to make us almost as powerful as the gods of the ancients.

We have deciphered the physics and the laws of creation to harness the same power by which the Sun can light our cities or turn them to ash. We understand the mechanisms of life in great detail. We can manipulate the very molecules of which we are made, DNA, to cure disease and aging or create weapons that can wipe us from the face of history. Soon we will be faced with the technology to build *better* people or repair anything that ails us. We are tackling immortality and the complex ethics of how we impact our fragile ecosystem.

We have made unbelievable and potentially devastating advances in war, from the handheld stick to a single button that can launch unimaginable horror across the world in minutes.

We have evolved as a society into a layered system. Those who have financial resources are able to benefit from our growing knowledge. At the same time, billions desperately cling to meaningless, dangerous, and depressing lives.

So what have we, as people, achieved?

We have more power than maturity. We are selfish. We are still tribal, hording our triumphs to our own ends.

We have the power to do better. We can make life on our planet easier. We can be more compassionate. We can look at our fellow human beings as brothers and sisters.

But we don't.

Science is the pure pursuit of knowledge. Ethics is often an afterthought. Wernher von Braun was asked whether it bothered him that his incredible advances in rocketry were used to kill the innocents. He is reputed to have responded, "I only build them. I do not decide where they go or how they are used."

The scientists in the Manhattan Project struggled with the ethics of building a weapon capable of heating a city to the temperature of the Sun's core in a few seconds. But they built it anyway.

We have the power of rationalization.

"If we do not build it and use it before the Germans do, we will lose the war."

The Germans blew our rationalization by losing the war before we finished the bomb. So we came up with a new rationalization.

Using the bomb to force Japan's surrender will "save" millions of lives. We thought that once the emperor saw the power we had created, an invasion of Japan would become unnecessary. A good rationalization, but many of the project's scientists wanted to use the weapon on a non-civilian target to convince the Japanese leaders that we could crush them.

But we had only two bombs. If they did not respond to the initial non-civilian demonstration, we might have had to bluff them into thinking that we had enough bombs to blow them into the Stone Age.

So we bombed Hiroshima.

In the confusion that followed, we dropped the second bomb on Nagasaki.

The Japanese surrendered. Science had delivered victory. But the costs were dramatic. Hundreds of thousands of civilians were vaporized, burned, or doomed to slow agonizing deaths from cancer and radiation sickness. We doomed generations to mutations from gamma-shattered DNA.

Now consider that the two atomic bombs were mere firecrackers compared to the next generation of hydrogen bombs, known as thermonuclear weapons. By the late fifties, both the United States and the Soviet Union went on a massive building spree of bombs and intercontinental ballistic missiles (ICBMs). Hundreds of billions of dollars were spent producing enough technology to kill every person on Earth ten times over. What kept each side from using its weapons? A policy called mutually assured destruction, aptly named MAD, maintained peace by convincing both sides that the other had enough retaliatory prowess to destroy the initial aggressor anyway.

Can you begin to imagine what the world would be like if we had focused the incredible level of mind and money on medicine, food production, or new forms of energy?

Scientists and armies need to be bound by morality and ethics in a more comprehensive way.

On the other hand, organized religion does not have a great record of accomplishment either. In the last few thousands of years, more people have died in wars and genocides under the banners of the world's great religions than in political conflicts. The small dispute between Christianity and Islam known as the Crusades continues even to the present day. Mass murders and persecutions under the sign of the cross must anger Jesus Christ himself.

The religions of the world should admit to a few simple facts.

If they truly believe that God exists, they must admit that there is one God.

The Hebrews, the Christians, and the Moslems all come from the same philosophical womb—Abraham. The Jews and the Moslems both stem from Abraham's sons, and thus are cousins!

How has the belief in one God and his covenant with the first peoples who accepted and honored his uniqueness, been perverted to the point where brothers kill brothers and invoke the name of the one God as justification?

If God exists, what would he think about this behavior?

Indeed, through his prophets, we have been given instructions as to how to live in peace. We have the Ten Commandments, the Old Testament, the gospels of Christ in the New Testament, and the Koran.

Have too few people actually read these books?

What part of "Thou shall not kill" is difficult to understand?

Imagine what the world would be like if we believe the Word of God and behaved according to their teachings?

What if we treated our fellow humans with love and respect? What if we shared the advances of technology and the derived wealth with everyone in the world? What if we diverted money from weapons and wasteful extravagance and used it to raise the quality of life for all God's children?

Earlier I pointed out that the Lord's Prayer includes "your kingdom come, your will be done, on Earth as it is in Heaven." If we really followed God's will and behaved as we have been directed, I have no doubt that the Earth would be more like heaven.

The next hundred years will bring the human race to a great crossroad. Our knowledge will grow so that we can conquer biology and be able to cure all diseases. Aging itself will have been cured. Solving the theory of everything will enable physicists to create almost infinite energy. We will be able to open wormholes and traverse the universe, and perhaps even cross into parallel universes. We might even be able to travel in time.

We will have the powers of a god in our hands. But we are not gods, we are human beings. We are flawed. We are too immature for such power. While one branch of the crossroad will bring us to heaven on Earth, the other will lead us to hell. Misdirected biology could create viral DNA machines capable of destroying all life on Earth. Physicists are attempting to create conditions akin to the beginning of the universe. A new big bang could rip space-time apart and destroy the world.

People who do not believe in the existence of God think that humanity is on its own. Without a benevolent guiding hand, left to our own devices, one would have to be pessimistic about our chances to survive our own shortcomings. In a random, violent universe, one can only depend on luck or chance for a positive outcome.

Because I believe that God exists, I am optimistic about our chances.

When President John Kennedy send American Navy ships to intercept Soviet freighters bringing nuclear missiles to Cuba, our high school sent us home early with the expectation that we were on the verge of a nuclear war. We did, in fact, get closer to the button being pushed that day than at any other time in history. As we left school, we said good-bye to our friends for what may have been the last time. On my subway ride home, I realized that we were not given any homework. I can still feel the chill of what that could really mean. My dad came home early as well, and I remember huddling together in front of our black-and-white TV watching the news.

My father used to tell my brother and me, "History happens one day at a time." That night he talked quietly of having seen this mood before as word of Hitler's invasion of Poland spread through his town in 1939.

I can still taste the tension in the small living room.

We sat at the edge of the end of the world.

But it did not end.

At the last minute, Khrushchev backed down, the ships turned back, and the world survived.

In response to our heartfelt prayers, God does take care of us.

As a little boy, I was angry with God for allowing the Holocaust to happen and for not protecting my Jewish family from evil. My mother lost her arm in a concentration camp. I later came to understand that my very existence depended on everything that happened to my family happening exactly in the way that it did.

I wanted to ask God whether or not he was involved with me personally. Many philosophers have asked this question in some form or another. Did the Creator create the universe and then stand back and watch how everything turned out? Was God the great clockmaker? Or is God involved in every event, every life on every planet in every galaxy in the universe?

Do we have free will? Or does God know how everything will turn out? Is the future fixed? If so, how can I be held accountable for my actions?

Does God really care or even notice what I do?

I believe our study of quantum probability yielded a definitive answer to all these questions. A quantum multiverse model contains the outcome of every choice in every situation in every place in the universe. One reality is that the Soviets did not back down, and the world ended on that day in the early sixties. There is a reality in which my mother died in a concentration camp, and thus I was never born. There is a reality in which Hitler died of pneumonia as a small child and the Holocaust and World War II never happened, and thus my parents never met, and again I was never born.

I am here because everything that happened to get me here did happen. You and I live in a reality that made us who we are. It could be that God is not personally involved in my life other than providing the framework that allows the existence of universes in which I am possible.

In probing the nature of the soul, we came face to face with what might be a very personal connection between the Creator and us, namely the created. If the soul is a thing different from the body and separable in origin and existence, then we may be a part of God Himself!

If the soul comes from God, and is given to us at birth, and becomes the self that we carry through life, then perhaps it is our connection to God.

This is what I believe.

My soul is me.

It exists in the same reality outside of time in which God exists.

Time is a perceptual artifact that we construct while we are alive.

When I am no longer alive in this universe, my soul continues to exist with God outside of time. When my body dies, the connection between my soul and my reality ends. Time and space end for me. My soul returns to its origin, to the presence of God.

> The Lord is my shepherd, I shall not want;
> He makes me lie down in green pastures.
> He leads me beside still waters; He restores my soul.
> He leads me in paths of righteousness for His name's sake.
> Even though I walk through the valley of the shadow of death, I fear no evil; for You are with me; Your rod and Your staff, they comfort me.
> Surely goodness and mercy shall follow me all the days of my life; and I shall dwell in the house of the Lord forever. (Ps. 23, King James Bible "Authorized Version," Cambridge Edition)

The purpose of my soul is to record everything I am; everything I have ever thought, said, or done; every experience; every emotion; everything that I ever learned.

My soul has touched my mother's face, my wife's heart, and held the hands of my infant children. It has cried at my parent's grave and smiled when my son threw a great block in a high school football game.

My soul is me.

When my soul returns to God, I believe it will carry everything that is me. It will bring the sequence of my life back to the entity that dispatched it.

Is there a heaven? Is there a hell?

I believe that when we die, we take with us the sum total of what we are.

In the movie *Ghost*, the character played by Patrick Swayze *steps into the light* and tells Demi Moore, "You get to take the love with you."

If you lived a life filled with love and goodness, then that is what you will take with you. You will be able to spend eternity based upon the warmth of that love and goodness.

That sounds like heaven to me.

If you lived a corrupt, evil life, filled with anger and pain, then that is what you will spend forever being. What a great definition of hell!

I believe that a few souls have entered mortal bodies with a memory of this exalted state of being. This is why I became a Christian. Based on my studies and the messages brought to us by Christ, I believe that he was such a soul, the Son of God.

If I were such a soul, I would understand that man is only partially corporeal. I would be aware of a father who either created distinct souls or shared part of Himself.

You and I are thus blessed.

Christ tries to tell us of this other existence, of this connection to the Creator. He tells, in John 14:1–4:

"Let not your hearts be troubled; believe in God, believe also in me. In my Father's house are many mansions; if it were not so, would I have told you that I go to prepare a place for you?

"And when I go and prepare a place for you, I will come again take you to myself, that where I am you may also be" (King James Bible "Authorized Version," Cambridge Edition)

When we die, we will join him in our Father's house of many rooms. He tells us not to fear death. He tells us that we need only to look at him and believe in what he is saying to find our way back to our Father.

Powerful stuff.

Christ came into our reality to tell us that heaven and hell were of our making. He provided guidelines for us to follow. He knew that we would be much better off in eternity if we lived a life according to the guidance of the Father. His parables expose the foibles of cherishing the transient wealth of this world at the expense of the eternal peace to come.

This is why I became a Christian.

I believe that my soul will return to the realm of God. I believe that I will take with it the love and joy that I have shared with my parents, my wife, and my children. I believe that these experiences will be just as real to me in my room in heaven.

I will see my parents again.

I will kiss my wife for the first time again and again.

I will watch as my children are born, learn to walk and talk, and then learn to talk back.

They will be real to me.

I do not fear death.

Instead, I cherish life and will continue to add to the goodness it offers. I will study and teach, I will earn and share my wealth, and I will spread peace rather than conflict.

I will return to God and give Him a high five for the great job he did creating the universe and making me "me."

It is, after all, what I was created for.

CPSIA information can be obtained
at www.ICGtesting.com
Printed in the USA
LVOW04s2054120816
500060LV00016B/174/P